Don't Tell Me To Relax!

ONE TEEN'S JOURNEY TO SURVIVE ANXIETY (AND HOW YOU CAN TOO)

Sophie Riegel

INDIE BOOKS INTERNATIONAL

ISBN-10: 1-947480-46-4
ISBN-13: 978-1-947480-46-9
Library of Congress Control Number: 2019931433

Designed by Joni McPherson, mcphersongraphics.com
INDIE BOOKS INTERNATIONAL, LLC
2424 VISTA WAY, SUITE 316
OCEANSIDE, CA 92054

www.indiebooksintl.com

To my brother Jake:

Thank you for listening to me when I felt like no one else would understand. Thank you for knowing that whenever I said, "I just want to be alone," I really meant, "I'm lonely. Please don't leave." Not only are you my brother, but you are also my best friend. Watching your confidence gave me the courage to write this book. Without you, this never would have happened.

Table of Contents

Preface vii

Part I. Me 1

    Chapter One: Problem 3

    Chapter Two: Getting Help 13

    Chapter Three: Diagnosis 19

    Chapter Four: Backlash And Coming Out 31

    Chapter Five: Anxiety and Death .45

    Chapter Six: The Demons in my Colon 61

    Chapter Seven: Second Diagnosis and Medication 79

    Chapter Eight: Effects Of Medication 91

    Chapter Nine: Hitting Rock Bottom 107

    Chapter Ten: A New Beginning .121

    Chapter Eleven: Journal Entries .135

Part 2: You 149

    Chapter Twelve: Facts vs. Myths about Anxiety 151

    Chapter Thirteen: For Parents 161

    Chapter Fourteen: For Teens 171

    Chapter Fifteen: Resources 177

Appendix 183

    Acknowledgments 185

    About the Author 187

Preface

When I was younger, maybe ten or eleven, I started to feel like I was different from everybody else. Not because of anything in particular; I just had a gut feeling that something was off. My friends all seemed so carefree. And I had the weight of the world holding me down.

Then I was diagnosed with obsessive-compulsive disorder. And trichotillomania (that's pulling out your own hair). And then generalized anxiety disorder. And then panic disorder.

Since then, I've been on a roller coaster, with plenty of ups and downs. Downs like being bullied, feeling the side effects of new prescription drugs, feeling hopeless, and even being physically paralyzed from panic right before one of the biggest athletic events of my life.

What were the ups? Getting an accurate diagnosis; finding supportive friends, family, teachers, and therapists; becoming the junior with the highest GPA in my high school; becoming the national champion in the racewalk; and learning to embrace my anxiety.

Oh, yes—and one more up. Writing this book.

Part one of this book brings you along on my journey from despair to diagnosis and treatment, and what I experienced along the way. Part two of this book is about you, whether you're a teenager or someone who lives with or works with teens. It highlights how to advocate for yourself, where you can turn to when you feel like you're all alone, personal advice from my mom to other parents, my advice for teens, and helpful resources.

I have a feeling that as much as I felt I was different from everyone else, I'm not. I have come to learn that when it comes to living with anxiety, I'm not alone. And now, you don't have to feel alone either.

Sophie Riegel

September 2018

PART 1

Me

Chapter One
Problem

It's the middle of fifth grade. I'm ten years old. And I have no idea what I am doing at Rachel's house. We're not friends. I know she has Mr. R for math, but that's it. When she invited me for a sleepover at her house with five other girls, I said yes reflexively, desperately wanting to be someone I wasn't, someone who didn't get nervous around her peers, someone who didn't sit home alone on the weekends.

Within minutes of arriving, we're sprawled out on the basement carpet, eating pizza and playing Truth or Dare.

I feel my stomach tighten. I do not want to play. I want to go home.

"Truth or Dare?" Rachel asks Carly.

"Dare," Carly says with a mischievous grin.

"I dare you to text Mark and tell him you like him."

Carly doesn't hesitate and texts away.

Carly then turns to me. "Truth or Dare?"

I want to say, "Pass," but I'm nervous that she and the other girls will give me a hard time, so I say, "Truth," too afraid of "Dare."

"What's your biggest fear?" she asks me.

"Glitter."

She looks at me like I have three heads. The other girls start to giggle.

"What?" I ask, feeling my face turn red.

"You're scared of glitter? That's ridiculous!" Carly says, and bursts out laughing.

I wish I could call my mom and have her pick me up now, but I don't want them to make more fun of me, so I laugh along with them and pretend to be OK. Even though I'm surrounded by other girls, I feel completely alone.

A few hours pass, and it's time for bed. I go to the bathroom and put on my pj's because I don't like changing in front of other people. I find my way to the hot pink and purple room where everyone has set up their sleeping bags. I crawl into my sleeping bag and face away from the girls so they can't watch me sleep.

When I wake up in the morning, the girls are staring at me, hysterical.

"What's so funny?" I ask, sitting up, confused.

"Nothing," Carly says, stifling a guffaw.

"Look in the mirror," Rachel says, prompting the other girls to howl, the kind of uncontrollable laughter that's so loud and contagious it gets you in trouble in a library.

I jump up and run to the bathroom, holding back tears. I can barely breathe. *Did they draw a mustache on me with a Sharpie? Did they shave my head? What is so hilarious?* I shut the door behind me and look at myself in the mirror. I scan my body, hair, and then face. That's when I notice it. A shiny green speck. I try to rub it off, but it won't budge.

OMG. OMG. OMG. Please come off. Please come off.

I move closer to the mirror to get a better look and to see if I can pick it off with my fingernails surgically, like playing the game Operation. I manage to get it off, only to realize it's one of millions.

My entire scalp is covered in green glitter. I let out the biggest scream of my life and don't stop yelling. My heart feels like it's exploding out of my throat. I want to punch the mirror. I try to scratch the glitter out of my hair and off of my skin, but it won't come off. I dig my nails so deep into my skin, I start to bleed.

(Fifth grade Sophie didn't know about OCD. She didn't know about panic attacks. She also didn't know that people could be so mean.)

I storm back into the room, hyperventilating and sobbing at the same time. The girls are pointing at me and clutching their stomachs from laughing so hard.

"Why would you do this?" I yell. "It's not funny!"

I want to kick myself for playing Truth or Dare the night before.

"It's just glitter. Chill," Carly says, rolling her eyes.

I'm crying so hard I can barely breathe.

"Relax," Rachel says.

"Don't tell me to relax," I say through tears.

Just then, my dad pulls into the driveway. I grab my sleeping bag and leave without saying goodbye. I get in the car, put on my seatbelt, and try to catch my breath.

My dad takes one look at my face and asks what happened. After all, I am bleeding from my head.

"They. Put. Glitter. In. My. Hair," I say, barely able to get the words out, feeling the tiny sparkles creep and crawl on my skin.

"OK," he says, not really understanding, but caring. "When we get home, I'll help you get it out. I'm so sorry they did this. Try not to let this ruin the rest of the day, OK?"

"Thanks, Dad," I say, taking the first real deep breath I've had since I woke up.

"Let's go home. I'm sure Jacob will give you a big hug when you get home," he says.

Jacob, my twin brother, is waiting for me when I get home. He wraps his arms around me and lets me wipe my snotty nose on his sweatshirt.

"Thanks, Jake," I say.

"No problem," he says, smiling at me.

———

That night, I lie awake in bed, crying, thinking about all the reasons these girls would do something so cruel. *Did Rachel invite me over just to have someone to make fun of? Did they all hate me? Did they think I was weird? Were they jealous of me because I got 100 on that really hard test? Were they getting back at me? Did they think I was a bitch because I mostly keep to myself? Were they trying to teach me a lesson? Were they sending me a message? What did I do to deserve this?* I feel silly and stupid and can't understand why I, captain of the basketball team and star student, am in this situation in the first place, all because of my fear of glitter. I don't understand. Or maybe I do and I just don't want to admit that I am being bullied. *It has to be my fault. What is wrong with me?* It's 2:00 a.m. and my pillowcase is soaked. I lift my red fleece blanket off of my body, get up, tuck my stuffed animal, Lammy, back into bed, and make my way to the top of the stairs, praying for my mom to help me.

Please come, Mom. Please. I don't know what's wrong with me. Help me.

Holding on to the banister, I clench my fist, hoping she will hear me crying and come.

I wait fifteen minutes, staring into the darkness, feeling completely lost and alone.

Just as I decide to go downstairs to get my mom, I see a shadow moving.

Oh no. Is someone there?

The shadow stops moving.

Is it a man? A robber? Is he going to shoot me? What is happening?

I reach for the light switch and stop.

If I turn on the lights, I'm an easier target.

I reach around in the dark and grab the closest thing to me to protect myself: a towel. I turn on the lights and run back into my room. I turn around to see if someone is chasing me, but the shadow I thought was a man is . . . *a freaking plant.*

By now I have completely forgotten why I wanted to go downstairs in the first place. I untuck Lammy, close my eyes, and become one with the dark.

——————

Sixth grade: I start cracking my neck. All the time. My mom is concerned (it's the overprotective Jewish mother in her) because she has a tic disorder and gets a shot in her neck every three months to control the involuntary movements. She doesn't tell me this, of course. She just watches and waits. When she sees it's a habit I can't break, she drags me with her to her own neurologist appointment under the guise of "running a few errands."

We sit in the waiting room and listen to a random guest on *The Ellen Show* talking about sloths until the nurse finally calls my mom's name.

My mom is perched up high on the big, scary patient's chair as Dr. T enters the room. He shakes my hand, and all I can think is, *I hope he washed his hands.*

"Your mom is going to get a shot in her neck," he tells me, as if to say, "You might want to close your eyes."

I start to cringe at the thought of a long needle going into my mom's body.

What if the needle is infected? What if the doctor puts the needle into the wrong spot and my mom becomes paralyzed?

"If you don't want to see it, you can go into the waiting room," he says.

"Yeah, I'll wait outside," I say.

"Wait. Could you take a look at my daughter's neck?" my mom asks Dr. T, afraid I will leave the room and never come back.

Ha! "Errands"? Very sneaky.

"Sophie has been cracking her neck a lot, and I'm worried. Honey, can you show the doctor what you have been doing?"

I tilt my head to the right, feel and hear a solid crack, lift my head back up, tilt it to the left, feel two deep cracks, lift my head back up, and feel satisfied.

The doctor looks down at his clipboard as if it's magic and has every answer to every question ever posed written on it.

"Are you able to stop doing it?" he asks.

"No."

"Then you have a tic, a compulsive movement."

"Just like me," my mom says, with a sad sort of smile. "Is this tic bad for her neck?" she asks.

"If it doesn't hurt her, it's not bad for her," he says.

I don't like having a tic even if it's not bad for me. I hate not being able to stop cracking my neck even though it feels good. And I wonder if there is more that I can't control. I hate that there is so much wrong with me.

_____

In seventh grade, I start having intrusive and violent thoughts about my favorite teacher, Ms. X. She's in the middle of the ocean surrounded by sharks. They're attacking her, ripping her apart. I see her dismembered, bloody body float in the water. I try to shake this image from my mind, but another awful scenario pops up. I see Ms. X running away from an active shooter. I picture her lying on her classroom floor, blood spilling out of her chest, no one there to help her.

During every class, I raise my hand and ask if I can go to the bathroom. I need to make sure she is OK. Standing on my tippy-toes, looking through the window of her door, I see her in front of the chalkboard, teaching, moving, breathing. She's alive. I wait for a few seconds until my heart rate slows back down to normal and return to class. This doesn't just happen one day; it happens every day. And I can't stop it.

My close friend, Jessica, a tenth-grader who is also very close with Ms. X, tells me about her anxiety one day and says that she has OCD—obsessive-compulsive disorder. I've heard of it before, but only from some TV shows where there is a character who is a neat freak. As Jessica is speaking, telling me about herself and her fears and compulsions, it's as if she's describing me. Our specifics are different, but I feel some relief. Maybe there is a name for what I have, and maybe, just maybe, someone can help me.

I go home that day and Google: "Signs of having OCD."

The first link I click on tells me that having OCD is *very* serious. "If you wash your hands too much, you can strip them of the healthy bacteria and your body won't be able to fight illnesses."

I wash my hands a lot. What if I get sick and then kill my entire family from the sickness? Am I sick right now? I'm going to die and kill everyone!

"One sign of having OCD is worrying constantly about catching a deadly disease and/or that you will contaminate others with your germs."

Uh-oh. Is Google reading my mind?

"An intense fear that something horrible will happen to a loved one."

Like Ms. X.

"Irrational fears."

Glitter.

"Many people with OCD are self-harming."

I Google: "Self-harming."

"Self-harming can lead to institutionalization. Many people in mental health institutions have attempted to commit suicide."

My heart is racing so fast I fear I might take flight and smash into the ceiling.

I type "OCD and suicide" into the search bar.

The first line I see is: "People with OCD are ten times more likely to commit suicide than the general population. Actively thinking about suicide (sometimes called suicidal ideation) also appears to be relatively common among people affected by OCD."

I don't want to be institutionalized and commit suicide. I'm just a kid. I just want to be "normal"—whatever that is.

Chapter Two
Getting Help

After diagnosing myself with OCD, I decide to tell Ms. X. I trust her and think she will understand. But what am I supposed to tell her? I can't say, "Oh, by the way, I definitely have a mental illness that my parents don't know about, and I haven't actually been diagnosed by a doctor, but yeah, I'm sure I have a problem. Oh, and did I mention that I am ten times more likely to commit suicide?"

Sitting in my bed, I conclude that I probably need to say something else, and I spend the next several hours trying to craft the perfect conversation.

Should I just come out and say, "I have OCD"? Or better yet, "I think I have OCD"?

Or, "Want to take a guess who has OCD?" Or I could be honest and say, "I think I have OCD and I'm really scared about what I read online about it. I don't know what to do."

I grab my journal from the shelf above my bed and get a freshly sharpened pencil. I write down all of the combinations of what I could say. It's like a puzzle that I need to solve. And I love puzzles. But as soon as I start writing, images start to appear in my mind.

I see Ms. X walking down the street. A bomb explodes right in front of her. Her limbs are scattered all over the sidewalk. The image replays in my mind, but this time, I'm there with her, screaming at her to get out of the way every time. I scream at the top of my lungs, but she doesn't hear me. I close my eyes, as if that will somehow make the image go away. When I open my eyes, I realize that I have snapped my pencil in half. Dripping with sweat and exhausted from my thoughts, I crash hard and fall asleep.

When I wake up the next morning, I get dressed and go downstairs to eat breakfast. My favorite is waiting for me: my dad's special chocolate chip pancakes (made with the not so secret ingredients: overripe bananas and, of course, love). Any other day, I would eat ten pancakes, no problem, but today, I don't feel like eating anything. I take one bite and immediately feel repulsed.

"I'm not hungry," I say to my dad.

"Uh...OK," he says, sounding a bit confused. "You OK?" he asks.

"I'm fine."

On our way to school, my queasiness amplifies.

Maybe I shouldn't tell Ms. X about my OCD. Maybe I should pretend I'm sick. I mean, it wouldn't totally be pretending. I don't feel well.

A block away from school, I feel as if I am going to throw up.

Why am I so nervous? I haven't been this nervous ever. What is going on?

I walk into school, go to my locker, and pretend everything is all right.

In Ms. X's class that day, I walk up to her and ask her if I could talk to her during lunch.

"Is everything OK?" she asks.

"Yes. I just want to tell you something."

"OK. Meet me in my room at lunch." She smiles at me and I sit back down, feeling a bit better.

The next period, I sit at my desk and I can feel the metal bars digging into my thighs. My legs are shaking. I can't focus. I stare at the clock, not understanding how time could be going by this slowly. I don't notice that my mouth is wide open until a fly flies in.

Ew, gross.

I start to cough and ask to be excused.

As I start to drink from the water fountain, I see Ms. X in the hall. I quickly hide behind a door so she won't see me. After making sure she is gone, I turn around and go back to class.

So strange. Why am I acting like this?

During lunch, I walk to Ms. X's room.

"What's up?" she asks me.

"Um…I'm not sure how to tell you this. I'm a little nervous."

"Are you OK?" she asks me, concern in her voice.

"Can you turn around while I tell you?"

"Sophie, what's going on?" she asks.

"Please just turn around. I'll explain," I say.

"OK."

After a few minutes of stalling, I finally spit it out, "I have obsessive-compulsive disorder, and I keep worrying about your safety.

I really care about you, but thinking about you makes me anxious. I can't fall asleep because I worry that you are going to die a horrific death. I am so sorry. Please don't judge me. I just don't know what to do."

Her back is still turned to me, and she is not responding.

This was a bad idea. I've made a terrible mistake. Do school floors ever just open and swallow you? Because that would be a cool feature right about now.

"I'm fine, sweetheart. I promise you. Try not to worry about me," she finally says. "What do your parents think about this?"

I realize I probably should have told them first.

———

After school that day, Ms. X walks toward me in the hallway. "Can I talk to you for a minute?" she asks.

I stop breathing for a second.

Is she going to tell me that I'm insane or that she doesn't love me anymore? What if she decides never to talk to me again?

"Sure," I say, acting cool, like I hadn't just admitted the most personal and scary thing to her hours earlier.

"Would you feel comfortable talking to the school psychologist with me? I would be there the entire time, and we would talk to her together."

"What would we talk about?"

"I think she can help us come up with some strategies to reduce some of your anxiety. Does that sound OK?"

I almost burst into tears, not from fear this time—from relief.

"Sure. Thanks for being so understanding and for not judging me," I say, taking a deep breath.

When I get home that day, my mom and I drive to get frozen yogurt. It is two-for-one day, so of course we have to go. In the car, I tell her I need to have a serious conversation with her. It turns out that telling people that you need to have a "serious conversation" with them really scares them. I then ask my mom to guess what I am going to tell her. Apparently, that isn't such a fun game for parents to play with their almost teenage kids.

(To this day, I still tell my mom to guess what I am thinking when I am nervous to tell her something. I do it because if she can guess it, then I don't actually have to say it. It is kind of like when you want to break up with someone, so you decide that you are going to make them break up with you just so that you don't actually have to deal with confrontation. I highly discourage that method of breaking up with someone.)

Just as I start to work up the courage to tell her, we arrive at the frozen yogurt place.

"What flavor do you want?" the woman behind the counter asks me.

"Um…I'll have Reese's in a small cup please," I respond after a moment of hesitation, not knowing how I am going to build my courage back up again.

When we get back in the car, I stall for another three-and-a-half minutes, and then blurt out: "I was talking to one of my friends, and she was telling me about her anxiety, and it sounded very similar to how I feel. She told me that she has something called obsessive-compulsive disorder, and her thoughts are very similar to mine. I promise I am not making this up. Sometimes my anxiety is so overwhelming that I don't know what to do or who to talk to."

I'm afraid she's going to tell me I am fine, it's all in my head. That I'm too young to have a mental illness. Instead, her face softens, and her eyebrows rise in an arch of the most gentle concern.

"Honey, thank you so much for telling me. Guess what? I have it too. Let's plan to get you some help, OK?"

"Wait, you have OCD?" I ask.

"Yes."

"I never knew that," I say.

My mom reaches over and hugs me, making sure to avoid knocking over my precious frozen yogurt.

"We are in this together, my love," my mom says.

"Thank you for understanding and for believing me," I say, feeling my shoulders practically drop to the floor from relief.

"Why would I not believe you? I love you. You can always tell me anything. We are going to get you help and find a great therapist who will help you figure out how to cope with it."

Then she asks me how I diagnosed myself, which leads to a very long conversation about why I shouldn't use Google to do that.

Chapter Three
Diagnosis

It's a Tuesday afternoon when my mom drives me to my first therapy appointment. I'm very nervous to meet Dr. S and I wonder if she will hate me when she gets to know me. And then I wonder why I hate myself so much and assume the worst all the time. I just want to feel normal and pray that she can help me.

My mom and I walk up thirteen steep stairs, ring the buzzer, and wait for the door to unlock. The buzzer is so loud, and I am so on edge, I jump a little.

Who designed this for a therapist's office? I mean, why scare people who already have anxiety?

We walk into the waiting room and sit down on a lumpy yellow couch. The lighting is a bit dim, and there is a small table in the corner with magazines on it. Before I know it, a woman wearing a black cardigan, brown skirt, and black boots is standing in front of us, as if she had materialized from thin air. I squeeze my mom's hand. She squeezes back twice, which means that she isn't going to leave me.

"Sweetheart, breathe with me. OK?" my mom says.

"OK."

We breathe together.

Dr. S waits for a minute and then asks us to come join her in her office.

I gulp and put my hand on my chest to make sure I'm not having a heart attack.

My mom and I follow her down the dark hallway, make a left, and go into the first room on the right. I notice that the window is open halfway or closed halfway, depending on how you look at it. I can see pigeons on the roof. Out of the corner of my eye, I see a man standing on the roof. I worry he is going to jump and imagine him falling to his death, his bones snapping as they hit the concrete below. I put pressure on my legs to hide the shaking.

"Tell me a little bit about why you are here today. And before you start, you need to know that everything you say in here is completely confidential and I will not tell anyone else, including your parents if they are not with you next time, unless I feel like you are going to hurt yourself or someone else. OK?" she asks.

Am I going to hurt myself? Does she know I'm ten times more likely to commit suicide?

"OK, so, I've basically diagnosed myself with OCD, and I'm here because I want to know that I'm right," I say.

I start listing all of my symptoms and the diagnostic criteria.

Dr. S laughs, "You've clearly done your research."

I smile.

Then she asks my mom why she brought me here.

"So, first of all, when Sophie told me that she thought she had OCD, I wasn't surprised. It does tend to run in our family, and I have some anxiety disorders, but also, as soon as she told me, I started to notice some of her obsessive-compulsive tendencies. And Sophie and I had a conversation about it, and we both agreed that she doesn't need to live this way. She doesn't want to be anxious all the time, and I don't want that for her, either."

Dr. S looks at me as if she can really understand my pain and truly wants to help.

"You are absolutely right," Dr. S says. "Sophie, would you mind telling me about some of the obsessions or compulsions you feel you are experiencing?"

I begin to tell her the story about the glitter, and I go on to talk about my fear of red markers, germs, and so on. My mom chimes in quickly and reminds me that a lot of my anxiety stems from the fact that she is away for work a lot and I am scared of something happening to her when she is away.

"Yeah. You are right, Mom," I say. "It is really hard for me when you are away."

"What do you feel when your mom is away?" Dr. S asks me.

"Well, I constantly think that I am never going to see her again. Like, I think about her plane crashing or her being murdered in her hotel room. Does that sound crazy?"

"No, Sophie. It does not sound crazy. That actually sounds a lot like an obsession."

"So, does that mean I have OCD?"

"It doesn't mean anything for sure, but to me, it does seem like you may be suffering from OCD. And it sounds like you are suffering from separation anxiety with your mom as well. How do you feel about coming to see me regularly so we can work on this together?"

I look at my mom. She gives me an approving look.

"Sweetheart, I think this would be very helpful," my mom says.

"OK. Let's do it then," I say.

———

A week later, I go back to Dr. S, but this time, I go by myself.

As I press the buzzer, I prepare myself for a loud noise. When it doesn't come, I'm confused.

Did she forget I'm coming?

As soon as I uncover my ears, the door buzzes, and I jump.

Why does this only happen to me?

A few minutes later, I'm in Dr. S's office, and no amount of pressure can stop my legs from shaking. *Shouldn't I be feeling good because she's going to help me? Why am I so nervous? Now that my mom isn't here, is she going to tell me the truth—that she thinks I'm really insane and there's nothing she can do to help me?*

I scan her face. She looks open and kind like she did last week.

Sophie, calm down and just see how this goes.

"How has the last week been for you, Sophie?" she asks.

"Hang on, that pillow was closer to the other side of the couch last time I was here," I say. "Also, is that a new bracelet? And I'm pretty sure the last time I was here, there was a box of tissues on your desk."

"Huh, I didn't notice that, Sophie," she says. "You are quite observant."

I smile, not knowing if that was a compliment or an indication of a new disorder.

"So, how was your week?" she asks again.

Still looking around the room, I tell her that my week was OK.

"Is there anything you would like to talk to me about, since your mom is not here this week? Or do you have anything in mind that you would like to tell me?"

"I guess we can talk about my fear of germs."

"That's a great place to start. What would you like to tell me about it?"

"I don't want to be afraid of germs. I don't like feeling like I'm not in control. Sometimes I get so mad at myself because it's like I have two different voices in my head that are constantly fighting. I just want to go through a day without being anxious about everything."

"That makes a lot of sense. That is definitely something we can work on together."

"I kind of feel ashamed of myself," I say, suddenly feeling very vulnerable and wishing I could take it back.

"That is a completely normal reaction. I can understand why you feel ashamed, but I'm here to help you feel more in control, not ashamed. Does that sound good to you?"

"Yes, it does."

"Can you give me a specific example of your fear of germs?"

"I constantly think that if I touch a doorknob, since so many other people have touched it, I will definitely get sick."

"Do you think that you are really going to get sick from touching the doorknob?" she asks me.

"It's possible," I say.

"Do you think it is *likely?*" Dr. S probes.

"Probably not," I admit, reluctantly.

"OK. So, when you feel the urge to go wash your hands or avoid the doorknob, I want you to remind yourself that you just said that you probably will not get sick. Once you can start to listen to your rational voice, you can start to control your fear."

"That makes sense," I say, feeling some relief already. I can see how therapy is going to help me already.

————

The next week, my mom joins me again, wanting to know how she can better help me.

"It makes me sad that when I go away, Sophie worries about me so much. I don't want her to be in pain," my mom tells Dr. S.

"I don't want you to be sad, because then I will be sad. I just love you so much, and I can't imagine ever losing you," I tell my mom.

Dr. S smiles at us.

"You clearly have a very close relationship. What do you think are some strategies that you could use when your mom goes away to help you feel less anxious?" she asks me.

After twenty minutes of brainstorming, we decide that my mom would text me every morning and call every night. I immediately feel better with a plan in place, but there is still so much left to tackle.

"I have this teacher, Ms. X, and I really love her. Maybe it's related to the separation anxiety with my mom; I always think she is going to die. It's always violent and I find it really scary. It's easy to ask my mom to call or text and reassure me, but what do I do about this situation? My fear immobilizes me, making it hard to concentrate on learning."

"OK, so tell me more specifically about these thoughts," Dr. S says.

"We are going to need more than forty-five minutes," I say.

"OK, let's talk about it next time, and we can focus more on how to control your fear of germs this session."

———

I'm getting ready to head to my seventh session with Dr. S, feeling hopeful about my future for the first time in my life. I am really starting to make progress. Granted, I still have fears, but understanding them more is helping me to face them. As I am putting on my shoes, I glance over to see my mom writing out a check for Dr. S and I flip out.

One hundred and fifty dollars. That is so much money to pay every week!

Ever since I was very young, I have worried about money. Even though my family has enough, we are far from poor, and I have always had enough to eat, I have felt very uneasy about my parents spending money on me.

My mom looks at me and says, "We are going to leave in about five minutes for Dr. S. You ready?"

"Actually, I don't think I need her help anymore. I feel pretty good."

"What do you mean?"

"I mean that I don't want to go anymore."

"That's not an option, sweetheart," my mom says.

"I can handle this on my own. I don't need therapy anymore. Trust me."

"What is this really about?" my mom asks, not buying my lie.

"Nothing. I just don't need it anymore."

"Is this about money?" she asks.

Deny! Deny! Deny!

"Maybe. I don't know. I mean it's a lot of money."

"This is our job. This is why we work—to be able to give you not just things you want—like sneakers and summer camp—but things you need."

I feel like such a burden.

On the car ride over to Dr. S, I apologize for saying that I didn't need therapy anymore, when I really want to apologize for needing therapy at all.

————

It's been a few months of therapy, and I can already see a difference in my behavior. I only check on Ms. X once a day, my mom texts me while she's on business trips, and I'm not totally consumed by horrifying thoughts. Being back on track feels good.

One spring morning, I sit up straight in bed, crack my neck, old school style, and reach my hands up to wipe my spring allergy crust away from my eyes like I do every other morning. But, some of the crust just won't budge. Having flashbacks to the glitter situation and how the glitter was stuck to my head, I begin to panic.

NO, NO, NO, NO! This has to come off. OH MY GOD please come off!

My heart starts to race. Pinching my fingernails together around my eyelashes, I begin to pull the crust off.

OK. It's coming off. Thank god.

I continue to pull off the crust, but in the process, I accidentally pull out some of my eyelashes.

Why does that feel so good? Maybe nobody will even notice if I pull a few more.

I reach back up to my eyes, grab my eyelashes between my nails, and pull. I pull again, feel the pain, pull harder, feel the release of the lash, and with it, the pain goes away. My heart rate decreases.

The next day, I wake up hoping that there is more crust. As I reach my hand up to my eyes to check, I don't feel any crust. I don't care. I feel compelled to pull out my eyelashes anyway, crust or no crust.

A few weeks go by and I am still pulling. Soon, there are noticeable gaps on my upper lid.

"Sophie! What happened to your eyelashes?" my mom asks me when I come downstairs. She is clearly alarmed.

"Nothing. I think it's from my allergies. You know, there is always crust on my eyes when I wake up," I say, lying.

"Honey, allergy season is over," she says, skeptically.

"Well, I still have allergies."

Why am I lying?

I flip around and run back upstairs. My face is red with shame. I reach for my hair this time and pull out one strand at a time.

Pull, pain, relief.

Pull, pain, relief.

Pull, pain, relief.

I feel my entire body tingle, and I think I might actually be relaxed. I reason with myself: If I pull out more than ten hairs, I have a problem. I must stop at ten. I pull eighteen.

OK fine. Just don't pull more than twenty.

I pull twenty-five.

Last chance, Sophie. If you pull more than thirty, you have to tell Mom.

I pull thirty-four.

I reach up to my head and feel something smooth.

Oh My God. It's a bald spot. Did I really pull that much hair?

I quickly spiral into a panic.

———

At my next appointment with Dr. S, she asks me how everything is going.

"I'm OK. I'm not checking on Ms. X as much, and I have started to find ways to reduce some of my anxiety."

"That's fantastic. What strategies have you noticed work for you?"

Do I tell her about pulling my hair? Does she notice some of my lashes are gone?

"I think breathing and texting my mom and dad when I'm in school really help me."

"I'm glad you are finding something that is working for you."

I wonder if she would be glad to hear I'm pulling my hair. I mean, it's definitely helping reduce my anxiety. She did say that she wants that for me.

"Keep up the great work and I will see you next week," she says.

A few days later, I'm sitting in my room, watching TV on my phone.

What if the FBI hacked my phone and they can see everything I do?

I bring my hands up to my eyes and pull out a clump of eyelashes.

Is there someone watching me?

I look outside my window to make sure no one is there.

What if they are just hiding really well?

As my mind races, I keep pulling.

The corner lashes hurt the most. I like the way it feels; it distracts me from the thought that someone is outside, tracking my every move and plotting my murder.

Pull, pain, relief.

Pull, pain, relief.

Pull, pain, relief.

I look down and see my lap is covered in eyelashes.

Sophie! How could you do this?

So much for calming down. Now I am in a full panic. I know I have to tell my mom, or rather that she'll tell me when she sees me, but I am so scared. I am tired of being so scared.

I find my mom downstairs and burst into tears when I see her. "I'm sorry. I'm so sorry. I didn't mean to do this, Mom!"

"I know, honey," she says as she holds me tightly.

"Mom, I don't know what to do. I keep on hurting myself. I hate myself."

"Honey, have you told Dr. S about this?"

"No."

"That's what she's here for. I'm going to come with you to your next appointment and we can talk about this."

"I'm embarrassed. I don't want her to be disappointed in me."

"She will not be disappointed in you. None of us are. We just want to help you because we love you. Please let us help you," my mom says, almost in tears as well.

My mom lets me cry in her arms until I feel better.

At our next appointment, my mom tells Dr. S about what has been happening. I'm too ashamed to utter the words and keep my head down.

"Sophie, please don't feel bad. This is a disorder called trichotillomania. It's the recurrent, irresistible urge to pull out body hair. It's related to OCD."

Great. Now my OCD has a new cousin.

Dr. S tells me to write how I feel about this new diagnosis. When I'm in my room that night, I grab a pencil and write:

> My scalp burns
>
> I like the pain
>
> It distracts me
>
> Distracts me from the reason I pull
>
> Distracts me from the cloud above my head that is anxiety
>
> Distracts me from how sad I truly am
>
> Sad that my aunt lost her hair
>
> Fucking Cancer
>
> She wears a wig
>
> Hating every minute of it
>
> She prays for hair at night
>
> She cries and begs for hers to come back
>
> I cry as I pull mine out and think of her
>
> Running my fingers through my hair
>
> Or at least what is left of it
>
> Trichotillomania

Chapter Four

Backlash And Coming Out

It's December vacation. My midterms are done (yes, we have midterms in middle school), and I'm ready for a break. When my parents tell me that we are going on a cruise for vacation, I'm beyond excited. I pack every pair of goggles I can find, and I write a reminder to pack underwear (I have forgotten it in the past). I cannot wait to scuba dive, collect shells, learn how to surf, eat as much ice cream as I want, and crush some boys in basketball on the ship. And I cannot wait to try every single pool (there are *fourteen*).

Wait. What if someone pees in the pool? How clean is the boat? What if it is contaminated?

I finish packing my clothes and make sure to pack plenty of hand sanitizer as well. I know I will need it.

What if there is some kind of bird flu outbreak? There's no place to escape. Do people die on cruises? This could be a total nightmare.

I have the urge to Google: "Death on cruise" and "Mass sickness on cruise." I stop, reminding myself that Google is not my friend during times like these. I take a few deep breaths and think about what Dr. S told me to do: challenge my cognitive distortions.

Sophie, think. How likely is it for that to happen? I guess it's not that likely. But maybe I should pack more hand sanitizer just in case.

When I bring my bag downstairs, my dad puts his hand on my shoulder, "How are you feeling about going on the cruise? How is your anxiety?"

"I'm feeling OK. I brought hand sanitizer, so I'm all good."

"OK. Just let us know if you need anything."

"Honey, please come find us if you are feeling anxious. Dr. S said we can also call her at any time if you need to talk," my mom chimes in.

"Thanks, guys," I say, smiling, because I really have the best parents ever.

––––––

As soon as we board the boat, I spot a hand sanitizer dispenser and immediately feel better. *Now there's no way I will run out.* I walk over, push the dispenser, and out comes the sanitizer. Magic!

A few minutes later, all sanitized up, I spot a sign for a new waterslide.

"Hey Jacob, let's go check it out," I say to my brother.

"Hang on, guys," my mom interrupts. "Let's bring our bags to the room first."

We walk to the elevator, press the button for the sixth floor, and go up.

What if the elevator crashes and we die?

As soon as we get to our room—room 238—we set our bags down in the hallway and get our keys out.

"Hey, Sophie, can you open the door?" my brother asks me.

No no no no no no no. Do you know how many people have touched that door?

I stand there silently, imagining touching the doorknob, contracting a deadly disease, and killing my entire family. I picture my mom lying on the ground, coughing up blood, while the sores on her limbs start to explode. Her bones are now visible, and she can't breathe from all of the vomit stuck in her airways. Holes appear on her head, and her brain starts to ooze out. She's looking at me, and as her body starts to give up the fight, she says, "It's all your fault."

My brother looks at me like I have ten heads. "Sophie? The door? Please?"

Don't you understand? If I touch that doorknob, I will most definitely get that flesh-eating bacteria I read about on Facebook, and it will eat away at my skin and then you and mom and dad will get it, and I will have to watch you all bleed and crumble and die as my body disintegrates into a skeleton while I'm breathing. DO YOU WANT THAT?

Stop it, Sophie. Just stop it. What would Dr. S tell me right now? She would say that that is not likely to happen. OK, breathe. Breathe. You are not going to get some random, rare, flesh-eating bacteria.

"Sophie, can you open the door already?"

I realize I've just been standing there, staring at the doorknob. As I reach my hand closer and closer to the knob, I can hear my mom's last words: "It's all your fault."

I quickly jerk back. I can't bring myself to open the door.

"Can you open the door?" I ask my brother.

"Fine," he says, rolling his eyes.

———

Over the next few days, after using a napkin to open my door, I stop about every ten minutes to sanitize my hands and feel so much better.

"Hey, Soph. Do you want to go to the game room with me?" my brother asks.

Do you know how many snotty, slimy kids have touched those machines?

"I'm OK. Thanks," I say.

"*Pleeaaase....*" he begs.

"I don't want to go."

"Just for a few minutes?"

"Fine. Ten minutes."

What did I just get myself into?

We walk to the game room, and along the way, I stop to sanitize my hands three times.

"Jeez, Sophie. Who uses that much hand sanitizer?" my brother asks.

"I touched something dirty. But I'm good now."

When we get to the game room, my brother immediately runs to the race car game. I stand in the corner next to the hand sanitizer.

"Soph, come play me," my brother yells.

No. I'm not touching that.

"It's been ten minutes. I'm going back to the room," I say.

It had only been six minutes and twenty-one seconds.

———

After the cruise, I get home and start feeling sick. My nose is running, my stomach hurts, I'm coughing, and my head aches. When

I go back to school, I make sure to use hand sanitizer to keep myself from getting even sicker.

"Sophie, you should go home," the nurse says. "You are really sick."

She calls my mom to come pick me up. When we get home, my mom makes an appointment with the pediatrician for later that day.

"Have you been using a lot of hand sanitizer lately?" the doctor asks me.

My face flushes. I feel exposed, found out, caught. He's just busted me. For what, I don't even know.

"Yeah. I guess I have been," I say, hesitantly.

"That strips all of your healthy bacteria also and makes you more prone to getting sick."

Shit.

"You need to stop using the hand sanitizer. And take the next day off from school and just rest. OK?" he says.

"OK."

———

Now it's the first day back at school from being sick, and my anxiety skyrockets. Everything in sight looks contaminated.

It wasn't the hand sanitizer that made me sick. It was touching the dirty doorknobs! I just know it.

I see the doorknob on the English classroom door. I can't help but think about how the germs are going to kill me. And then I look to my right and see the hand sanitizer in the classroom.

Don't do it, Sophie. Be strong.

I resist the urge.

Next period is gym class. My teacher takes out basketballs and we start doing dribbling drills. I'm a very good basketball player, so my teacher asks me to demonstrate a crossover and the lefty layup. She tosses me the ball, and as soon as it touches my hands, I drop it, as if we're all of a sudden playing hot potato.

"Actually, I have to go to the bathroom. Can I be excused?"

I have to wash my hands immediately. (Hey—washing my hands is *not* using hand sanitizer.).

"Just do the demonstration, and then you can go," she says.

"Please. It's an emergency," I say.

She gives me an odd look, and then I give her *the* look. You know, the look that someone gives a teacher when she just got her period and needs to be excused.

"OK, be quick."

Wow, I can't believe that worked.

I go to the bathroom, wash my hands, and come back. I feel better until the other kids in my gym class start to pick on me.

"Hey Sophie, can you hold this ball for me for a second?" one kid asks.

"Can you ask someone else?"

"Why? Are you *scared?*"

"Fine. Give me the ball." As he hands me the ball, I start to panic. "Never mind, I have to go. Get someone else to do it. Or better yet, put the ball on the freaking ground. Ever thought of that?"

———

My fear of germs only escalates, and then my fear of red markers comes out, full swing. School starts to be a total nightmare for me.

I hold my breath as my Spanish teacher rifles through her purse. She's looking for a red marker; I know it. Not a black marker, which I would be totally fine with, but no—she needs a *red* marker. And she's wearing a white, ruffled blouse. I don't get it. I shut my eyes tight. I can't bear the thought of red marker getting on her shirt. In fact, I can't stand the sight of it at all.

Stay calm, Sophie. Breathe.

I clench my fist around my pen. I want to punch a hole through the wall next to me. I look back up at my teacher. All I see are hundreds of red lines covering her shirt. This feels like glitter, only it's not on me. It's not even on her. It's in my mind and I can't stop it.

I feel paralyzed. I can't move my legs.

What is happening to me? This is bad.

"Is everything OK, Sophie?" my teacher asks me as she and the other kids start to notice my panicking.

"Yeah, uh, could I get some water really quickly?"

"Yes, sure," she replies, her eyebrows raised in concern.

I hate the way she is looking at me. Like she thinks I'm a weirdo or some sad kind of a mess. And it's not just her. The entire class looks at me like that.

I stand up from my desk carefully. I feel like my knees are about to buckle underneath me. I slip my hands in the pockets of my gray hoodie and leave.

Walking down the hall, I stare at my neon green running shoes, trying not to make eye contact with anyone. I'm two feet away from the water fountain when I start to see red marker everywhere. Red marks on white shirts. Red marks on people's arms and faces. Red marks on the walls. It feels violent, more than intrusive. I can't stop the images.

I close my eyes and take a long sip of water, hoping the coolness will calm me, but I only see red, red, red, red, red, red, red, red, red, red.

I walk back into Spanish class almost in tears.

"Can you not use a red marker, please?" I ask my teacher.

"Why?" she asks.

"I have a weird fear of them and I really would rather you use some other color."

She looks at me with strange concern. "OK, no problem. Now please, sit back down."

Everyone is staring at me. They all know now. I am so screwed.

It's one thing to know I have OCD, but it's another thing to live with it. I want to call Dr. S or my mom, but I also want to learn how to deal with this on my own.

OK, Sophie. Here's the plan: Avoid red markers at all costs. No exceptions.

The next day, I'm walking down the hallway on the way to math class, and a classmate starts to come up to me.

"Hey Sophie," she says.

"Hey, what's up?" I respond.

As she walks closer to me, I notice her hand slip behind her back as if she is hiding something. When she gets to me, she quickly pulls out a red marker from behind her back.

You have to be kidding me.

"Here. I got this just for you."

I walk away as quickly as possible and desperately try not to cry.

Stay strong, Sophie.

Later that day, in Spanish class, someone raises his hand and asks the teacher if he can write the answer on the board. I don't think anything of it until he asks the teacher if she has a red marker that he can write with. I start to panic as the entire class stares at me.

Uh oh, don't freak out.

All these kids know that I am afraid.

Is anyone going to say anything? Is anyone going to help me?

No.

———

The bullying has gotten to a point where I am now made fun of by people I don't even know.

"Hey Sophie," some boy says as he walks toward me.

"Do I know you?" I ask.

"No. But I know you. And I think you are really cool. So cool that I got you a gift."

He pulls out a bag of red sharpies and hands them to me.

"What is this?"

"It's for you. I know how much you *love* red markers," he says with a smirk on his face.

I turn around and run into the bathroom, and burst into tears.

———

I'm standing at my locker, getting my things ready for next period, when I see Alicia, one of the most popular girls in school, approach me.

Wait, is she coming toward me?

I turn around to see if someone is standing behind me. Nope.

I flip back around right as Alicia walks past me.

Out of the corner of my eye, I see her wave.

Wait, did she just wave at me?

I raise my hand to wave back, but she gives me this odd look. That's when I see all of her friends looking at me, laughing at me.

Then, with no warning, she shoves me against my locker.

"Hey, don't push me," she says.

"I didn't push you. You pushed me!"

"Hey girls, you saw Sophie push me, right?"

"Yes, we did," they say in unison, as if they are in some kind of cult.

I grab my folder and textbook and head to class. As I walk by the "I hate Sophie" posse, I keep my head down.

"Push Sophie," one girl whispers.

"No, you do it," another girl whispers back.

I feel someone grab on to my backpack and shove me.

"Hey, red marker girl, watch where you are going."

I go home that day, hysterical.

"Mom, I can't do this anymore. These girls bully me every day!" I say.

"Who? What do they do?"

"Alicia and all of her friends. They call me names, push me around the halls, and get other people to bother me too. What should I do? I hate school," I say.

"Why don't we talk to the principal about this, OK?"

"OK."

The next day, I am called into the principal's office.

OK, Sophie. This is your chance.

"Hi, Sophie. I got an email from your mom saying that Alicia and her friends have been bothering you and pushing you around. This is obviously quite concerning, and I'm wondering if you would feel comfortable telling me your side of the story?"

I explain what happened, and feel my shoulders relax. It feels freeing to not take it anymore, to speak up for myself.

"Thanks for telling me, Sophie. I already spoke to Alicia," she said.

"What did she say? Are you going to punish her for this?"

"Actually, she denied everything completely."

"Ask the people who were there. They see it all the time."

"I already spoke with them," she says.

"What did they say?"

"They said that you are making this up to get her in trouble," she tells me. "Is there any part of that that is true?"

I burst into tears.

"They are bullying me. Every day, they call me names, they get other kids to push me around, they take my desk in class, and they think that just because they are popular, they can do whatever they want and get away with it. Why would I lie about that? I wouldn't make something up like that."

"I never said I believed them. I just wanted to get your side of the story."

"I told you my side. But you aren't going to do anything about it. It is them versus me, and you believe them."

"Sophie, you are a smart girl, which means you should know that I can't do anything about it if no one corroborates your story. I'm sorry. That's just how it is."

I storm out of the office, and I see Alicia and her friends in the hall smirking at me.

What did I do to deserve this?

———

Lying in bed, awake, sweating, I know I have to figure something out. I can't keep living like this. That's when it hits me. If someone were to have a visible, physical disability and other students teased her about it, the school would definitely recognize it as bullying, and hopefully do something about it. But because my problem is invisible—inside my head—my peers don't understand. They don't know I am wrestling with mental illnesses.

I have to tell everyone, but the fear of coming clean feels more overwhelming than a red marker encrusted in glitter. Yet the fear of not speaking up, protecting myself, and educating the rest of the kids is even bigger than that, if that's possible.

When I tell my mom what I want to do—essentially "come out" as having a mental illness—she suggests that I spend time with my therapist planning how to share my battle with my classmates. We eventually decide that I'm going to make a presentation in front of my entire grade.

———

I am fully prepared. I have notecards, a PowerPoint, a backup plan, and an extra change of clothes (just in case). Still, I am shaking.

Just picture everyone in their underwear, I tell myself.

"Sophie, feel free to start whenever you want," I hear my teacher say.

Oh crap.

I am standing at the front of our social studies classroom and all I can see are thirty faces staring at me, including all of the people who have bullied me. The windows are open slightly and I can hear the wind whistling. I want to leave, but I know I can't. I've come too far to give up now.

I take a deep breath and begin.

"Hi. You guys have known me for a few years, and there's lots of stuff that you know about me. But, today I'm here to tell you something that you don't know about me. I have OCD, which stands for obsessive-compulsive disorder."

Wow. I can't believe I just did that.

"Does anyone know what OCD is?" I ask the class.

I'm surprised to see so many hands go up.

"OCD is when you freak out if you touch something dirty, right?" one kid says.

"Someone with OCD would freak out if you had a bag of chocolate chips and there was one peanut butter chip in it," someone else says.

"That's not exactly what OCD is. Let me explain."

For the next twenty minutes, I explain what OCD is and how it affects me. I end by asking if anyone has any questions.

"So, when you use hand sanitizer, do you feel better? Does it cure your OCD?" one kid asks.

"Using hand sanitizer is the compulsion to my obsession about being contaminated by germs. When I use it, it temporarily reduces my anxiety, but eventually, the obsessions come back. It does not cure OCD. OCD does not have a cure," I say, feeling like an expert.

"So, what can we do to help you?" another kid asked.

"That's a really nice question. If you see me feeling anxious, instead of staring at me, just ask me if I need anything. If I say no, just respect that and let me deal with it myself. And, if anyone has questions for me that they don't want to ask in front of the class, feel free to come talk to me at any time."

After I answer the last question, my classmates all clap for me, and I feel somehow vindicated. Freed, new. For the rest of the day, kids come up to me and tell me how brave I am and apologize for ever having done anything to make me anxious.

I feel a strength inside myself that I have never felt before. I wish that strength translated to not being afraid of red markers, but at least for now, I won't have to deal with kids making fun of me for it.

Chapter Five
Anxiety and Death

Today is March 6th and it's my Aunt Nancy's birthday, so as our family tends to do, we celebrate with food (more specifically, carbs!).

"Happy Birthday!" I say to my aunt as soon as I see her in the kitchen. This is a special birthday for her, since she has just found out that the rare cancer she was diagnosed with two years before is finally in remission.

"Thanks Sophus!" Aunt Nancy says as she opens up her arms for a hug. She is the only person I let call me by this nickname because she does it with so much affection. I start to worry to myself "Who will call me Sophus if her cancer comes back and she dies?" And then I tell myself that today is a day to focus on celebrating. I take a deep breath and I smile at her.

Every time I see her, it's so obvious how much she loves me. I hug her and then hug my cousin Wendy who is standing right behind her.

"Sophie, can you go get Jacob from the basement please?" my mom says.

"Sure."

When Jacob comes upstairs, we sit down, getting ready for a massive carbo load (even though I'm the only competitive athlete in the family).

The bagels come out and naturally, we start talking about how grateful we are to be celebrating the birthday of such a wonderful woman.

"Let's go around the table and say one thing that we love about Aunt Nancy," my mom suggests.

"I'll go first," I say. "I love your enormous heart, but more importantly, I love your fashion sense. Your mismatched socks are always fun to look at and they are super funky, just like you."

"I love how resilient you are. After a long battle with cancer, you came out on top. I'm so glad that you are here and healthy and happy. You are such a fighter and I love you," my mom says.

OK, so she topped me. But hey, I'm only fifteen. Give me a break.

"I'm so glad to get rid of this fucking wig," my aunt says.

No one is surprised by her profanity. That is what she is known for.

"Enough of this, I want to eat!" my aunt says.

Nobody argues. We happily dig into the bagels and ice cream.

"Are you going to make your famous mac and cheese for the next family dinner?" my brother asks my aunt.

That's a dumb question. Of course she is going to make it!

"Do bears shit in the woods?" she responds.

Well played, Aunt Nancy.

My brother starts to laugh so hard that I think he's going to choke on his own spit. At first I get scared for him. But then I realize that if he chokes, I can have his ice cream.

After we all finish eating, I go upstairs and I become quite distracted by the mess on my desk. It makes me feel anxious to see the sticky notes and scraps of paper in piles on my desk. I feel a deep knot in my stomach looking at it, and I start to clean it up when I hear my mom yell: "Sophie, Aunt Nancy is leaving."

"OK," I say back, not planning to go downstairs to say goodbye.

Sophie! What are you doing? Stop cleaning your damn desk for a minute so you can say goodbye! What if this is the last time you see Aunt Nancy?

My anxiety starts to kick in, so I go downstairs.

As Aunt Nancy is getting her coat on, I can't help but admire how beautiful she is, inside and out. An unexpected wave of emotion comes over me.

"Bye, see you soon!" I say to her as she gives me a tight hug. "I love you."

"I love you too, Sophus!"

I suddenly have a very strange feeling that this is going to be the last time that I will see her.

Sophie, she's fine. Everything is fine. Nothing is going to happen to her. This is just your anxiety talking. Remember how Dr. S told you that you need to control your thoughts? Now is the time to practice that.

Quickly, I run up to my room and have the sudden urge to look out my window at Aunt Nancy until I can't see her anymore. I watch as she gets into her light green car and drives away. I imagine being in the car with her, admiring her purse that is made of bamboo, and getting distracted by how much I love the smell of her car. I wish I could explain what it smells like, but the only way to describe it is that it smells like Aunt Nancy: strong, sweet, and unlike anything I had ever smelled before. In her car, I feel comfort. I feel like the smell washes away all of my worries.

———

Around 3:00 the next morning, I wake up in tears.

I get out of bed, tuck Lammy back in, and go downstairs to my parents' room. I don't hesitate this time. I walk into their room and tap my mom.

"Mom, I need you," I say through tears.

"What's going on?" she whispers.

"I had a nightmare about Aunt Nancy and I can't fall asleep. Will you come upstairs with me please?"

"OK, one second."

My mom lifts up her covers and slowly follows me up to my room. She gets into bed with me and holds me as I continue to cry.

"I'm scared that she is going to die. I always have these visions that I'm speaking at her funeral. I can't stop imagining it and it makes me feel like I'm evil or something. My mind replays my funeral speech over and over again and when I try to distract myself, it gets louder. And then the speech turns into my speech for your funeral. I don't know why this is happening. It scares me," I say.

"It makes sense that you are scared. And I'm sorry this is making you so anxious," my mom replies. "Is this something we can talk to Dr. S about? I think she would have some insights."

"OK. But can you still stay for a few minutes please?"

"Sure."

"Mom, I love you. I don't know what I would do without you," I say.

"You are going to be stuck with me for a very long time. I promise."

"But how do I know that you aren't going to die tomorrow?"

"You don't know that. But if I die, you have to trust me that you will be OK. I know it doesn't seem that way but you are so strong."

"I don't want to live without you," I say, crying harder.

"I know, honey. I don't want to live without you either."

I soon fall asleep in my mom's arms.

————

The next week is an ordinary week. I go to school, run at track practice, and hang out with my family. As I'm studying for my Biology exam, I hear a knock on my door.

"Come in," I say.

I see my dad and my brother standing in the doorway.

"What's up?" I say.

"I have to tell you and Jacob some news."

My heart races.

Who died? What's happening. Where's Mommy?

"Aunt Nancy is in the hospital. She fell down the stairs and hit her head," he says.

The world seems to freeze around me.

"Wait," I say. "She's not in the hospital for her cancer?"

"It's not her cancer," my dad says. "She had an accident."

Is she going to die? It's my fault!!! I was the one who dreamt about her dying and now she is going to die! If I hadn't thought that, it wouldn't be happening.

"Is she going to be OK?" I quickly respond.

"I think she will be OK. Try not to worry about it. I will let you know when I have more information."

I can see the fear in his eyes, but he knows that if he tells me that he's scared, he would be giving me every reason to be scared too. As he leaves the room, my brother moves closer to me. He notices that I am starting to cry, so he reaches over, gives me a big hug, and tells me that everything is going to be OK.

"Do you want me to stay in here with you?" he asks me.

"No. I just want to be alone. Thanks though," I say. As he walks out of the room, I call his name.

"Jacob," I yell. He turns around, a bit startled, and asks me what I need.

"I just wanted to tell you that I love you," I say.

"I love you too, Soph," he says with a smile on his face.

As soon as he is out of sight, I grab my favorite fuzzy red blanket and curl up in my bed. I put a pillow over my face so that nobody can hear me sobbing.

This is all my fault. She's in the hospital because of me.

I just sit there, thinking about how the world is so big, and how I seem so small. I think about how insignificant I must be and I wonder what the point of life is if we are all just going to die anyway.

What's the point of loving people if we are just going to end up losing them in the end?

I feel like I have so many unanswered questions that nobody else seems to think about.

What if none of this is real? What if life is just a game and I'm losing? What if I die tomorrow? Where will I go?

That night, I go to sleep at 6:00 without any dinner. I don't feel like eating while my aunt is in pain.

My dreams haunt me while I sleep. I can't stop picturing Aunt Nancy falling down the stairs over and over and over and over again. I wake up soaked in my own sweat and tears.

Why is this happening? What did I do to deserve this? What did she do to deserve this?

Over the next few days, I try not to think about what is going on, but I see Aunt Nancy everywhere I look. When I look at my English book, all I can think about is how Aunt Nancy would have corrected the grammar in it. When I look outside, all I see are trees and flowers that pale in comparison to Aunt Nancy's garden.

The week seems like it will never end. Seconds feel like minutes and minutes feel like hours. As time goes by, I lose all hope.

After school on Friday, I go to track practice. I feel much better after running a few miles and clearing my head. When my dad comes to pick me up, I can see that his face is red.

Please be a sunburn. Please. Not tears.

"How was your day?" he asks as I put my backpack in the trunk of the car.

"It was good. How was your day?" I ask, hoping that he will say it was fine.

"It was fine," he says. I breathe a sigh of relief.

When we pull into the driveway and open the door, my dad starts to say something: "Come to my room. Mommy and I want to talk to you."

No. Oh no. Please be something good.

As I walk into my parents' room, I see my mom sitting on her bed, wrapped in a blanket.

"Hi honey. How was your day?" she asks.

"Fine," I say. "What's going on?"

"Come sit, honey," she says.

"No. I don't want to," I say aggressively.

"We have something to tell you," she says.

My heart rate increased.

"I already know," I say.

"Know what?"

"I know this is about Aunt Nancy. She's not going to survive the accident, is she?" I say as I start to panic.

"No, honey. She's not doing well. She's not breathing on her own and her brain is swelling. We, as a family, have decided to take her off the respirator," my mom says with tears in her eyes.

My heart sinks.

This has to be some kind of nightmare. Wake up, Sophie!

I stare at the floor, unable to make eye contact with anyone. For once, my mind goes blank.

I put my face in my parents' comforter and begin to cry. I feel my mom put her arms around me as she begins to cry. I can't imagine a life without Aunt Nancy.

How can I live in a world where things like this happen? Maybe I don't want to live at all.

The statistic from the internet flashes in my head: "People with OCD are ten times more likely to commit suicide than the general population."

I quickly get myself together, knowing that this kind of thinking is not going to help anyone.

"What if we take her off the respirator but she would have survived had we left her on it longer? How can we just kill her? What if she just needs some more time? How can we do this? I don't understand! We can't just do this to her. She could live. Please, we have to wait. We can't do this," I say.

I begin to cry again.

"Honey, even if she did wake up, she wouldn't be Aunt Nancy. She would have serious issues. She probably wouldn't be able to walk or talk ever again. I know this is hard. But, do you think Aunt Nancy would want to live this way? Do you think she would want to be non-communicative? Do you think she would want us to have to take care of her all the time? Sweetie, Aunt Nancy is already gone. She's only being kept alive because she's on a respirator, but her soul isn't there anymore. She wouldn't want this for herself."

"I know. But..." I say. "It's just so hard."

We sit there on the bed, covering our broken hearts in warm blankets. My mom holds me as we cry on each other. My heart pounds so hard, I think I'm going to die too.

At least if I die, I will be with Aunt Nancy.

That night, I cry myself to sleep. I wake up in a pile of my own hair. I don't even remember pulling it out. I go down to my parents' room and crawl into their bed with them. I can't be alone with my thoughts.

Anxiety and sadness have mixed into a toxic concoction that I am forced to swallow. I have never felt pain like this before. Knowing that I have said my goodbyes and that I will never tell her that I love her again makes me nauseous. She will never come to my wedding. She will never meet my children. She will never watch me grow up and aspire to be like her. She will never see me defeat the beast of anxiety.

The next morning, my mom asks me if I want to go to the hospital to see Aunt Nancy one more time before we take her off the respirator.

"Am I going to be scared?" I ask my mom.

"It's a little scary because of all of the tubes, but she still just looks like Aunt Nancy. You don't have to come. No one will be mad at you," she says. "We are going tomorrow in the morning. Sleep on it and decide in the morning. Whatever you decide, I will support you."

That night, I can't fall asleep. Images of Aunt Nancy flood my mind. But the images are all covered in blood. I go downstairs again and get my mom.

"Is everything ok?" I hear my mom whisper from her bed.

"No," I say. "How can this be happening? I keep on thinking that it's a dream and that I will just wake up from it, but I know I won't."

I start to cry again.

"Come here, honey," my mom says.

I walk over to her bed, climb in, and cry on her. She holds me tightly, and I feel her try to stop herself from crying too.

"I'm scared, but I need to go to the hospital tomorrow," I say.

"OK. I will be with you the entire time, and if you decide you want to leave, we will leave. No questions asked. OK?" she asks.

When I wake up the next morning, I feel very uneasy. I'm anxious about going to the hospital and I start to have a panic attack.

"I don't know if I can do this," I tell my mom.

"Let's breathe together, OK?" she says.

"OK."

After breathing for a few minutes with my mom holding my hand, something become very clear to me: panic and fear are temporary, but love is forever.

I decide that I don't want fear to control me anymore. I refuse to let it come between me and Aunt Nancy. I refuse to let it stop me from saying goodbye one last time. I refuse to be scared anymore.

When we get to the hospital, I feel my stomach drop. My mind starts to spin out of control and I have to squeeze my mom's hands to keep myself from screaming out in pain from my broken heart. I clench my teeth together to keep myself from yelling at the doctors for not saving her. I want to let out all of my anger, but I hold it in for Aunt Nancy's sake. I don't want to remember being angry and sad the last time I see Aunt Nancy.

When we get close to Aunt Nancy's room, I freeze. I watch my family standing around her, and I'm thinking about how badly I wish I could have prevented this. The flourescent hospital lights seep into my skin and all I see is white.

I put my hands over my face and start to cry. My knees buckle under me and I go down. My dad turns around and sees me crying on the floor. He comes over to me, hugs me, and tells me that I don't have to go any closer to Aunt Nancy if I don't want to. I have never seen someone dying in front of my eyes before.

Slowly, I build up the courage to go closer and sit next to her bed. With my heart pounding, I put my hand in Aunt Nancy's. Her hands are not as cold as I imagined they would be, but it still shocks me. She feels lifeless. I imagine her being swallowed by death, only to realize that there is no heaven or hell; there is only darkness. I don't want Aunt Nancy to be trapped in the darkness alone, so I tell her that I am here for her. I tell her that she will not be forgotten.

"I'm going to make you proud," I whisper in her ear. "I promise."

I don't know if she hears me, but even if she doesn't, she already knew.

I sit with her until I have to leave. Doctors come in and out, but I stay. My grandpa reads the sports section of the newspaper to her, hoping that she would be so angry by how badly the Mets were doing that she would have to wake up. Finally, it is time to go.

With tears dripping down my face, I let go of Aunt Nancy's hand.

"I love you," I say, one last time. I turn around, holding my mom's hand, and leave.

In this moment, it feels like the world has just collapsed and we don't know if we are going to survive. When we finally walk out of the hospital, the sunlight starts to burn my eyes.

How can it be so sunny outside when there is so much darkness in my heart? How can the world just go on like nothing happened?

That night, as soon as I find out that my aunt was taken off the respirator and had succumbed to her injuries, I run up to my room, pull out my sock drawer, and begin mismatching all of my socks in honor of Aunt Nancy. Despite the fact that mismatching my socks gives me anxiety and triggers my OCD, my love for Aunt Nancy is so much stronger than my fear.

After disordering, or as I like to call it, "Nancifying", my socks, I pick up my journal and begin to write. "I'm speechless," I write. That's it. That's all I write. There are no words to describe the loss. There are no words to describe what it is like to know that as hard as you try, there is no bringing her back. There are no words to describe how it feels to know that I will never get to see her smile again.

Over the weekend, my mom tells me that I can write a speech for the funeral. I spend hours trying to figure out the perfect way to honor Aunt Nancy. When I can't think of anything, I decide to call her house to hear her voice on the voicemail recording. After that, my speech becomes very clear.

I pick up my pencil and write: "First, I just want to say that I hope this speech is grammatically correct or else Aunt Nancy might haunt me forever.

"I used to think that people were immortal. What I now know is that people may not be immortal but love is. My love for my Aunt Nancy will never die and will never stop growing. Her love was contagious. It was immeasurable and infinite. She had such an enormous heart and I feel so lucky to have been in it. Her kindness and strength were inspiring and her courage and lovingness was unlike anything I had ever seen before.

"When I went into the hospital to see her, I told her that she would not be forgotten. I said that she had an impact on everyone she met. I also told her a secret. I said that I am envious of the fact that she lived so confidently and happily and I can only hope to be half as confident and happy one day. She makes me want to be a better person. I remember that every summer I would go over to her house to pick raspberries. That was my favorite thing to do. She used to make fun of me because I would eat them all before they got into the bucket. My face and hands would be stained with that purple raspberry color. She would laugh and tell me that my hands might be stained for the rest of my life. When we went inside she would pour some of the raspberries that she picked into my bucket when I wasn't looking just so that I had more to bring home. I always knew that my bucket felt a bit heavier.

"Most people may not know this but a few years ago we had a planking competition. It's a bit embarrassing to admit this but I got my butt kicked. I think I lasted maybe a minute and a half and she was still going at four minutes. At some point I said to her that she had made her point and that I will never underestimate her again. I am very competitive but I never felt so happy losing before because it made Aunt Nancy smile. I would say that I let her win but everyone would know that I am lying. She was strong and she knew it.

"A wise man once wrote, 'Don't cry because it's over; smile because it happened.' I am here today smiling because I had the honor of sharing my life with a person who saw the world in the most special way. It is nothing but a gift to be able to say that I loved and was loved by Nancy Strong. If I had a flower for every time I smiled when I was with Aunt Nancy, I would have a garden almost as amazing as hers.

"Most people never get to say goodbye. I feel so lucky that I got the chance to tell Aunt Nancy that I love her one last time and that she will always be in my heart. I have no doubt that she heard me but even if she didn't, she already knew. Today, I have lost a part of myself. A part that came solely from the joy that Aunt Nancy brought to me. But I know that I will find that part again as we continue to remember her as the beautiful person that she was. My prayer for her now is that her soul lives on to embody someone worthy of it. She deserves nothing less. If I grow up to be a fraction of the person she ever was, I would consider myself to be absolutely the luckiest person. Today, the world loses an amazing human being. But, heaven has just gained an angel. Aunt Nancy was an angel sent to this world with a mission to make everyone smile and make sure that they know that they are loved unconditionally. Mission accomplished, Aunt Nancy. Mission accomplished."

I don't know if I believe in heaven, but do you know what I believe in? I believe in love. And I believe that Aunt Nancy is watching me now. And someday in the future, she will see me beat anxiety. I don't know how or when this will happen, but I am determined to make it happen. For her.

Chapter Six

The Demons in my Colon

I need to get a picture of you for your first day of tenth grade. Come downstairs please," my mom yells up to me.

I'm not ready. I can't find my deodorant, and I'm sweating a lot.

"You almost ready?"

"I need a minute, Mom."

I'm nervous about the first day.

This year is so important. Valedictorian is on the line.

"Mom, can you come upstairs please?"

My mom opens my door.

"What's going on?"

"I don't want to go to school. Can I stay home please?"

"Why? What happened?"

"I'm just not ready."

"Is this about your grades?"

"I guess so. I mean this year really matters for if I will be the valedictorian or not. And I'm really nervous that I'm going to screw up."

"I understand. But right now, worrying about this isn't going to help you become the valedictorian. And just so you know, Daddy and

I don't care if you are the valedictorian or not. Only you do. No one is going to be disappointed in you."

"OK. I just really want it."

"I know. Let's talk about this more later."

"Fine."

My mom hugs me.

"Can we take the picture now?" she asks.

"Sure."

After we take the picture, my mom drives me and my brother to school.

"I don't feel well."

"You are going to be OK. Trust me," my mom reassures me.

"Can I call you during lunch?" I ask.

"Of course, honey."

As my mom pulls up to the school, I start to feel uneasy.

"Sophie, I'm proud of you. You are incredible. Don't forget that."

"Thanks, Mom. I love you."

"Love you too."

My mom pulls away. I feel a sudden jolt of coldness. The gray building is more uninviting than ever.

My brother puts his hand on my shoulder. "You good, Soph?" my brother asks me.

"Yeah. Just nervous."

"You got this. Have a great day."

"You too, Jake."

———

I walk into my fifth-period class very excited.

It's math; I love math.

"I'm Ms. F. The first thing that you need to know is that there will be more rigor and challenges than last year. You should be prepared to work harder and more independently to make connections both in class and on tests. If I teach you two things separately, it is completely fair game to have a question on the test that involves both. This class is hard."

Oh, no. This class is going to be impossible.

"I've been teaching since I was your age. And I have multiple degrees in all types of mathematics." She picks up a piece of chalk and draws a dot on the blackboard. "When I first met my professor, this is how he greeted us: He picked up a piece of chalk, drew a dot on the blackboard, and told us that, compared to him, we know the area of the dot and he knows the area of the entire blackboard. So, this is how you may feel compared to me. I know a lot."

Everyone laughs, except me.

When I get home that day, I tell my parents about Ms. F.

"I'm scared of my math teacher," I say.

"I'm glad you have someone to challenge you," my dad responds.

"That's exactly what you said about my fourth grade teacher. And she ended up hating me."

"No, no. I'm sure Ms. F is nothing like that teacher."

"But what if she is?"

"We will deal with that *if* that happens," my dad says.

"Fine. But I don't trust her."

"Honey, you can't live your life like this," my mom chimes in.

"But also, what if she gives me horrible grades? You know how much I care about my grades."

"I understand that, but you are in control of your grades," my dad says.

"You don't know that. You don't understand what I go through everyday. I have nightmares all the time about my teachers failing me. You don't understand how much pressure there is to be perfect all the time. Everyone is constantly comparing themselves to me and when I screw up, I never hear the end of it," I say.

"Sweetie, I know how hard this is for you. And I wish there was more we could do to help you feel calmer about going to school. How about we go to Dr. S and talk to her about this?" my mom says.

"Fine. We can go."

"And can you give Ms. F a chance please? What if she ends up being your favorite teacher, but you miss out on that opportunity because you don't trust her?"

"I'll try."

The next day in school, Ms. F announces that we have a test coming up.

"It's going to be challenging. If you think you cannot study and still do well, think again."

I don't like this.

———

It's the day of the test, and I've spent hours studying. I ask some friends who have Ms. F for first period if the test was hard.

"It was impossible!" one girl says.

"I definitely failed," another girl says.

Shit. I can't do this.

I call my mom. "I don't feel well. I have to take this test in an hour and everyone said it was so hard. I think I'm going to throw up."

"Honey, you are going to do as well as you can. You've studied and there is nothing more you can do now. Trust yourself."

"But I don't feel good. My stomach really hurts."

"Take some deep breaths, get some water, and know that you are really good at math. You got this. And if it doesn't go well, we will deal with it then."

I walk to my next class trying to control my shaky legs. I sit, pull out my notes for math, and continue studying. My teacher starts to teach, but I'm not paying attention. My stomach really hurts.

"Can I go to the bathroom?" I ask my teacher.

"Sure."

I go the bathroom and have diarrhea. And then more diarrhea.

"Are you OK?" my statistics teacher asks me when I come back to class after being in the bathroom for half of the period.

I nod and sit back down.

I look down at my notes again. When I look back up, everyone is staring at me. I realize my legs are shaking so fast that the floor is vibrating.

You've never seen anyone shake their legs? You need to get out more.

I smile awkwardly, and try to stop.

"Can I be excused for a minute?" I ask my teacher.

"Sure," he says.

I get up, push in my chair, grab my jacket, and walk out. My stomach is growling so loudly that I swear the teacher on hall duty can hear it. I walk slowly to the bathroom, and as soon as I open the door, I make a sprint for the closest stall.

Not again.

I lose everything, except maybe my vital organs and my fears. I start to cry and look at my watch. I have four minutes until my test.

This cannot be happening now.

I muster up the strength to stand and slowly walk to my math test.

"Are you all right?" Ms. F asks me when I walk into her room. "You look pale."

"I'm not feeling so well. I think I just lost half of my body weight in the bathroom."

Why did I say that? She did not need to know that.

"You will be OK," she says.

A few minutes later, Ms. F passes out the test.

"I'm going to vomit," I say accidentally.

The whole class looks at me. The people next to me move their desks over slightly.

"The test is now out. Any talking is considered cheating," Ms. F says.

Breathe.

When the test ends, I walk out of the room. I feel relieved, but also terrified.

Did I get that question wrong? Maybe I got the entire test wrong.

The next morning, Ms. F breaks the news to me as lightly as she possibly can.

"You did not do as well as I think you would have liked to," she says kindly.

Please just tell me.

"Did I fail?"

"No, you got an 86. I know that this grade doesn't represent you. I know that you will do better on the next one. Try not to let this bother you too much. I really believe that you are capable of so much more and you will learn how to be successful in my class."

Wow. That's really nice. She thinks I can do better.

"I'm going to study differently next time. I think I know what I need to do now," I tell Ms. F.

"I have confidence in you."

"Thanks."

————

In Dr. S's office, I tell her about my math test. "So, I just took a math test and I got an 86. I don't know what happened, but I was so nervous before. And I was in the bathroom for almost half an hour pooping my brains out."

"What made you so nervous?"

"I don't know. I guess I've never not done well on a test before, so when people told me that it was hard, I got scared."

"And what were you thinking that caused you to be so nervous? Because clearly, your body had a reaction to the anxiety."

"I was thinking that I was going to fail. And I want to be the best at everything I do. I also didn't want this class to be the reason why I'm not valedictorian."

"OK. So, there are a few things here that we can talk about. First of all, one thing that we can do is to start tracking your thoughts when you get anxious like this. If we can figure out what thoughts are triggering your body to have such a physical reaction, we can start to change those thoughts. Next time you have a test, I want you to write down what you are thinking. And when we do this for a little while, we can start to look for patterns."

"OK. I can do that."

"And another thing that you mentioned was valedictorian. Why is that such a big goal of yours?"

"I want to be the best. I want to show people that, despite everything I've gone through, I can still come out on top. And it would be nice because so many people have been mean to me about being smart. I want to show them what I can do. If I'm not valedictorian, people will make fun of me forever."

"So, is this more about other people than it is about you? Because your goals need to be for you, not for other people. If you want to be valedictorian because you are scared that people will be mean to you if you aren't, then that is not a good reason. But if you want to do it for yourself and because you earned it and worked hard, then that is something we can talk about."

"I guess I never thought about that before. I want it for both reasons, I guess."

"But is it worth putting this much pressure on yourself? I mean you are having serious physical reactions to the anxiety. You have two more years in high school after this. Is this what you want to go through to be valedictorian?"

"I don't want to feel this way. But I put in so much work, I can't imagine not being the valedictorian."

"Well if this is a goal of yours, we need to make sure that we go about achieving it in a healthy way. And you have to remember that a lot of this is out of your control. You cannot control how well other students do. And sometimes, you can't even control how well *you* do. There are always going to be hard tests that you may not do well on. Does it mean you won't be valedictorian? No. But we have to think of some strategies to handle the stress that comes with being an excellent and competitive student."

"You are right. What do you think I should do?"

"I think that you may need to think about talking to some of your teachers about your anxiety. And you also have to start to accept that this is mostly out of your control. No matter how hard you work or how much you study, you cannot say for sure that you will be valedictorian. The lack of control won't be an easy thing to accept, but it is something we need to work on. OK?"

"Yeah. Thanks."

"And most importantly, it is important to understand that, if you did as much as you could do to succeed, then no matter what the outcome, you should be proud."

———

A few weeks later, we have another test in math.

OK, Sophie. Think about what Dr. S said. You worked hard, but at the end of the day, there is nothing more you can do.

I go to school that day, nervous. My stomach is growling. The diarrhea comes early this time.

Why is this happening again?

I call my mom. "It's happening again. This is bad. It really hurts."

"This must feel really frustrating. I'm so sorry this is happening. Let's talk to Dr. S about this again, OK? But for now, just get through the test and then we will deal with it."

"Thanks, mom."

I hang up, still sitting on the toilet. I suddenly feel very nauseous.

I feel my stomach convulse. I vomit and feel calmer, but only for about a second.

I still have a test.

"Was this test harder than the last one?" I ask someone as I leave the bathroom.

"Yes," she says.

I run back into the bathroom and have more diahrrea. When there's nothing left in me, I get up and walk to my class, feeling like I'm walking toward my execution.

Ms. F hands out the test. I can't get the 86 out of my mind.

I take a breath and start the test.

Try as hard as you can; that's all you have to do.

———

That night, I sit in bed wide awake.

On question three, I think I accidentally wrote a six instead of an eight and I screwed up the entire question.

I clench my fists so hard and dig my nails into my skin. I start to bleed.

Damn it. Why do I do this to myself? I need a bandage.

I wrap my blanket around myself, get out of bed, tiptoe across the hall, and look for a bandage. When I can't find one, I go downstairs to another bathroom to get one. As I walk down the stairs, I hear them creak.

"Who's there?" I say quietly.

No one answers.

Why would a robber or murderer tell me if they were there?

I giggle at my stupidity.

If there is a murderer here, at least I won't have to find out my grade on my math test.

I shake my head.

That's an awful thought. Don't think like that.

I finally get the bandage and put it on my hand where nails had cut open my skin. I'm honestly shocked that after four years of biting my fingernails, my nails are long enough to cut through my skin. I go back upstairs, get into bed and fall asleep.

For the next few days, I bug Ms. F.

"Did you grade the test yet?"

"No. I will let you know when I do."

The test is all I can think about. I try to distract myself, but it's consuming.

A few days later in class, Ms. F announces that she graded our tests.

"A lot of you guys made the same mistakes. Many people forgot to set the equation equal to zero. And many people did not simplify the radicals."

She is definitely talking about my mistakes.

I put my hands over my face to cover up the panic.

"Are we going to get the test back today?" one kid asks.

"Tomorrow."

Tomorrow? Are you kidding me? I have to live like this for another day?

When class ends, I start to walk out of the class.

"Sophie, can I talk to you for a minute?" Ms. F asks me.

Oh no. What did I do? Did I fail the test? I definitely failed. She's probably going to tell me I should drop her class.

My heart is racing.

"So there have been some complaints that I want to talk to you about," Ms. F says.

"Complaints? About me?"

"Yes. Some students came to me and told me that they think you have an advantage when taking my tests. They think that you know the answers before you take the test. And I want to get your side of the story. I need you to be honest with me. Do you ask people for the answer before the test?"

Me? Cheating? Definitely not!

"Um. I don't ask people for the answers. But I do ask people if they thought it was hard or not. That's a lot different."

"You can't do that anymore. I trust you, but I don't want to have to report anything like this. Some people consider this cheating, and I think that you should just stop that now before you get in trouble."

Oh no. She's mad at me. I disappointed her. There's no coming back from this.

"I'm sorry. I never meant for this to happen. Are you mad at me?"

"No. I'm coming to you first about this because I trust you. And because I didn't want to assume anything."

"There's something else you should know," I say.

"OK. What is it?"

"You know what? I'm going to be late for my next class. Can we talk tomorrow?"

"You can't leave me like this. Now I'm worried about you. What's going on? I'll write you a pass for your next class."

"I'm not exactly sure how to tell you this. This is not an excuse for what I did but here's the truth. I have OCD. And I've been feeling overwhelmingly anxious before your tests. So, when I ask people how it was, it somehow makes me feel calmer. I know it's not an excuse. But I'm so anxious before your tests that I've been throwing up. Even though I've been going to therapy for three years, I still feel like this."

"Thanks for telling me. Let me think about it and we will talk tomorrow."

"OK. And can we keep this between us. None of my other teachers know about this."

"Of course."

I feel relieved, but also nervous.

The next day, we get our tests back. While she's handing back our tests, I start reciting the digits of pi in my head (yes, I know, I'm a nerd).

"Sophie? Come get your test," Ms. F says.

I'm not ready.

I walk to her desk. I swallow hard and feel my stomach turn over.

I wonder if she can hear my heart beating.

I look at Ms. F. She's smiling.

Is she smiling because I did well or because she doesn't want to scare me before she shows me my failing grade.

She stops smiling.

Oh no! Why did she stop smiling?

"Do I have to look at my grade? I don't know if I want it."

Please don't make me look. Maybe the fire alarm will go off.

She says something, but I don't hear it. I'm distracted.

"What?" I ask.

Oh, great. Now she thinks that I don't pay attention. Focus!

"You are going to want to look," Ms. F says.

For some reason, I don't believe her. I don't know if she knows that a 90 isn't good for me. Even a 95 would not be good for me. As I lean in to look at my grade, I start to panic. I see I got a 79. Then, I realize that I was reading it backward. It's really a 97.

"Great job," Ms. F says to me.

Yes!

When I get home that day, there's a voicemail for my mom from Ms. F. I can't resist playing it.

"Hi. This is Ms. F, Sophie's math teacher. I just wanted to call and say what a fabulous improvement she made on test two and I'm really impressed with how she stepped up to the challenge and has worked on modifying her studying needs to meet the rigor of class. So, I just wanted to touch base and say great job, Sophie. OK, thanks so much. Bye."

No teacher has ever called to congratulate me before. I cannot believe this. Ms. F is awesome.

————

The following week, Ms. F tells the class, "I know there is a typo on the test. It doesn't impact any of the answers, but for those of you who are OCD like me, I fixed it."

I cannot believe she just said that. After I told her about my OCD. My real *OCD.*

When I go home that day, I tell my mom what happened. "Ms. F made a comment about OCD. I feel like she completely disrespected me. And I trusted her. I don't know what to do."

"Sometimes people make mistakes. I make mistakes too. If you have a good relationship, maybe you should ask her about it privately. I bet she didn't mean to do that."

"But what if she did mean to do it?"

"If she did mean to do it, then talking to her will educate her even more. Why don't you try it out? You might be pleasantly surprised by her response. But you cannot be rude about it. Be direct but respectful."

"OK. I'll talk to her tomorrow. But just so you know, I'm really upset about this. I *hate* when people don't think about what they are saying."

"I know, honey."

The next day I go up to Ms. F. "Can I talk to you for a minute?"

"Yes. Is everything OK?"

"Not really. This is not easy for me to tell you. I don't know if this was intentional or not but yesterday you said something about OCD in class and I was offended."

"Oh my goodness. I didn't even realize! I'm so sorry. It just kind of came out. I wasn't even thinking about how you would react to that. I feel horrible. If you want, I can apologize in front of the entire class about misusing that term."

"No. That's OK. This is just between us. I just wanted to let you know. I'm not trying to make you feel bad. But it's important to me that the people who I trust know about my anxiety and know about some of the stigma and how that affects me. I'm not mad, I was just confused."

"It's very mature of you to come talk to me about this. Thanks for letting me know."

"You are intimidating sometimes, so this was hard for me. I'm glad you appreciate it as opposed to being angry."

"I intimidate you?"

"I'm scared of you sometimes. You are so smart and confident. I also have a lot of trouble trusting new people. Maybe it is my anxiety, or maybe it is something else. I'm not sure. But either way, I'm constantly worried that you will do something or say something that triggers my anxiety and that I will spiral out of control."

"Sophie, I'm so sorry. If I ever do say anything that makes you feel uncomfortable, just let me know and we can talk about it."

"OK. Thanks for being so understanding."

The next day, Ms. F comes up to me. "Can we think of some strategies we can use to help you go into tests feeling less anxious?"

"What do you have in mind?"

"If you don't mind sharing, what does your therapist tell you to do?"

"She's been sharing strategies with me for how to control my mindset. We've been trying to figure out what thoughts are setting me off."

"What does she say about your physical reactions?"

"We are still working on that."

"Would it be helpful if I gave you your test earlier in the day so that you don't have to stress about it during the day?"

"I don't want you to have to make special accommodations for me. I feel bad."

"Sometimes, it's important to ask for help. This is something you will learn."

"I don't know if that would help though. Can I think about it?"

"Sure. Also, if you don't mind me asking, are you taking any medication for your anxiety?"

Medication? I've never thought of that before.

"No. But I can talk to my mom about that."

I guess I have more to learn from Ms. F than just math.

Chapter Seven
Second Diagnosis and Medication

The day after talking to Ms. F, I wake up with a sick, gurgling stomach. It's the weekend, so I don't know why I'm anxious. My legs start to shake. I stand up, but they give out under me. I lay on the ground in a fetal position and close my eyes. My head is pounding. Concrete walls and metal bars enclose me. I reach out to touch the bars. The cold metal sends shivers throughout my entire body. *Why am I in prison?*

I look around for a cellmate or window and some kind of clue to help me know what's happening. The wall to my right is covered in blood. I run to the bed and flip my body to face the other wall. I start to cry. I feel so disoriented and out of control. I look down and notice my feet are filthy. I hope that's not blood. My big toe starts to dig into the wall. I must break through. I must get out. I hear a scream, and then feel something drip onto my forehead. I put my hand on my forehead to see what's dripping. Just then, the ceiling starts to crack.

Open your eyes, Sophie!

I can't move. The visions keep coming. I jump out of bed, run to the back wall and see hundreds of scratch marks from the person before me, trying to claw their way out. I fall to the blood-stained floor.

Open your eyes!

I start to feel like I have been here before. My knees fit perfectly into the dents in the floor and my fingernails match the scratches on the walls. When I finally muster up enough strength to get up, I realize that my clothes are soaked in my own sweat. My heart is racing fast and the room starts to get darker. I throw myself onto the bed before the lights go out completely. I stare at the dark ceiling for what seems like hours. My mind is empty and my body is numb.

Open your eyes, now. Now!

I'm surprised when I hear a guard walk toward me. I cannot see him, but I feel his presence, and it, too, feels familiar. I ask him where I am, but he does not answer. Instead, he opens my cell. I get up, dizzy and confused, and walk toward the cell door. The man disappears as I push open the door. As I step out, the lights turn on and I look around in disbelief. There are hundreds of cells identical to mine. And each of them has the same blood stains. Each of them also has a prisoner inside who looks eerily like me. At once, they all stand up and say "You survived again." And then instantly, they disappear. I blink and the cells are gone.

Open your eyes!

"It's OK, honey. I'm here," I hear my mom say.

I'm sitting on my bedroom floor, shaking. My mom is cradling me like a baby, rocking me back and forth.

"Breathe with me, honey, breathe," my mom whispers into my ear.

The feeling in my legs and hands come back. It's over.

"How long have I been here?"

"Ten minutes."

"How did you find me?"

"I came into your room to wake you up and I saw you like this. I knew you were having a panic attack."

"That was a bad one. Thanks for staying with me. I'm sorry if I scared you. I didn't know what was happening."

"That's what I'm here for."

"I had these weird visions that I was in a jail. I felt so scared."

"Let's talk to Dr. S."

"Actually, mom, can I talk to you about something?"

"Sure. What's up?"

"I'm so sick of feeling sick every day. Especially during tests. I've been throwing up and having diarrhea. I don't feel like myself anymore. As much as I try listening to Dr. S, I still feel like something is always wrong. What do you think about medication?"

"I think we should consider it. I mean, there's no reason for you to feel like this. How do you feel about it?"

"I'm nervous about it. I'm scared that if the medication works, I won't be myself anymore. My anxiety drives my success. I don't want to lose that. But, I also don't want to feel like I am going to die every single day."

"I understand that. Here's what I can promise you. If you don't end up liking the medication, you can always stop. And I think the medication would just stop the anxiety from feeling overwhelming. I think that it would calm down the voice in your head that is telling you that you have to be perfect."

"Thanks, Mom."

———

The following weekend, I'm watching *Criminal Minds* with my brother in the living room when my mom approaches me with a thick packet.

"Hey honey. I found a psychiatrist, Dr. G. Before we go, he would like you to fill this form out for him."

"I have to answer all of those questions?"

"Yes."

"Can you at least do it with me?'

"Sure."

My mom and I leave my brother to finish watching the show in the living room, and we head to the kitchen. She makes me a cup of tea, and we begin.

"OK. So, I'm going to read you a series of statements and you tell me if the statement is often true, sometimes true, or never true. Here's the first one: Can't concentrate."

"Sometimes true."

"Complains of loneliness."

"Sometimes true."

"Worries a lot."

Me? Worry? Never.

"Often true," I say, laughing.

As we continue, my mom starts to smile.

"Plays with own sex parts in public," my mom reads.

"You are kidding, right? You just made that up."

"No, I didn't. It says it right here. Why are you hesitating to answer? Is there something I should know?" my mom laughs.

"No. Never true."

"Plays with sex parts too much."

"All right, I'll finish this by myself."

"We are almost done. Let's just finish this together," my mom says.

"Has set fires on purpose to cause damage."

Maybe I don't need a psychiatrist. There are people out there who clearly need way more help than I do.

"Never true."

Jacob walks into the kitchen and sits down with us, clearly unable to handle *Criminal Minds* on his own.

"Is physically mean to animals?"

"Wets self during day?"

"I hope you know those answers, Mom."

"Has strange ideas?"

"Like making a peanut butter, tomato, and cheese sandwich (*my favorite*)?"

"I don't think this applies to you, honey."

"Do you get annoyed easily?"

"Do you feel insecure?"

"Do you feel hopeless?"

The questions continue.

"Do you have bowel movements outside of the toilet?"

Jacob starts to laugh uncontrollably.

"Are we done yet?" I ask.

"Yes, that was the last question."

"What are these questions for?" Jacob asks.

"The eye doctor," I quickly respond.

"Oh. OK."

Ha. He totally believed me.

"Wait. Why would someone need an eye doctor if *that* is their problem?"

My mom, with no hesitation, says "Maybe they just can't see that they are not in the bathroom and they need glasses."

Jacob isn't buying it.

After a few minutes, I tell Jake that the form is for a psychiatrist and he says he is thankful that I always keep my bowel movements inside of the toilet—even if sometimes I am too scared to flush in the middle of the night.

———

A few weeks later, my mom drives me to Dr. G's office.

"Hey, Sophie. Come on in," Dr. G says.

I walk into his office; he has sticky notes everywhere.

I think we are going to get along quite nicely.

Then I see granola bars under his desk. They are the same ones that I have. I trust him instantly.

My mom sits down on the leather couch with me.

"So. I'm going to get right to it. I don't want to waste any time. From speaking to your mom, here's what I know about you: You have obsessive-compulsive disorder, you have a habit of biting your nails, you pull out your eyelashes, you are very smart and capable, you have had a fear of germs, you are a great athlete, you have a twin brother, you go to therapy, and you have had many panic attacks. Is that pretty accurate?" Dr. G asks.

"That pretty much sums me up," I say.

"Mrs. Riegel, can you leave us here for a few minutes to talk?"

"Sure," my mom says, picking up her purse and walking out into the waiting room.

"Everything that you say here will stay between us, OK?" Dr. G reassures me.

"OK."

"What's the craziest obsession that you have?" he asks as he picks up a tennis ball from his table and plays with it.

"I don't know. Like flesh-eating bacteria? Or red markers?"

"Come on. That can't be the craziest."

"Can you give me an example?" I ask.

"Here's an example: I had one person tell me that they can't stop picturing themselves stabbing their mother. So, anything you say will probably not throw me off too much," he tells me.

"I have those thoughts sometimes. Sometimes I can't stop picturing myself stabbing my mom also. It hurts me to think about that. No matter what I do, the visions come back. They come when I least expect it, and I don't know what to do when I start thinking about it," I admit. "I also can't stop picturing myself falling off the top of a building or jumping off a bridge. I'm not suicidal, but these thoughts always come back. I never ever think about killing myself, but these thoughts confuse and scare me," I tell him.

He definitely thinks I'm insane.

"Do you think I'm crazy?"

"No. The person who has these thoughts is actually the least likely to carry out those actions," he tells me. "I'm not worried about you at all," he reassures me, and puts down the tennis ball.

"OK, so here's what I want you to do for me now. Tell me what you feel when you have a panic attack," Dr. G says.

"I feel like I'm dying. My heart races, my legs shake, and I feel like I'm paralyzed. My mind races a million miles an hour. Every time, I'm scared that I'll have a heart attack."

I expect him to start writing notes but he just listens and slouches further into his dark leather chair.

"When do they happen?"

"Usually right before tests. Especially math tests. But I've been having them more randomly lately."

"How often do you have a panic attack?"

"Maybe once a week or so."

"And if you could rank for me from least important to get solved to most important, how would you rank your OCD—those "crazy" thoughts that you have—hair pulling, and panic attacks?"

"Hair pulling, OCD, panic attacks."

"So, it's important to you that you don't have panic attacks anymore."

"Yes."

"How often do you feel anxious."

"All the time."

"Even right now?"

"I guess I'm fine now. But I'm distracted."

"So, when you have downtime and are bored, is that when you get anxious 'randomly'?"

"I guess so."

"I want you to keep track of when this happens. It makes sense that when your mind isn't busy, you are anxious. There is nothing to distract you from your intrusive thoughts."

"Yeah. That makes sense."

"And can you tell me about your hair pulling?"

"What do you want to know?"

"Where do you pull the hair from?"

"My eyelashes and my head, mostly."

"And how often do you pull?"

"I think it's gotten better but probably a few times a week."

"When you pull, how many hairs do you pull?"

"I'm not sure. It depends."

"Have you ever pulled enough to leave a bald spot on your head?"

"Yes. A few times."

"Does your mom know?"

"No."

"Why not?"

"I covered it up mostly."

"Can we tell her?"

"Can *you* tell her?"

"Sure. And how do you feel before and after you pull?"

"I feel anxious before and after I feel relieved. I don't want to pull. I feel bad about it."

"Can you stop if you try?"

"I don't think so."

"And that's why it's a disorder. Let's bring your mom back in."

"OK."

My mom walks back in.

"Sophie and I have been talking and she told me a little bit about her OCD and her hair pulling. We want you to know that it has been bad enough at times that she's had bald spots that she's covered up. And in addition to that, it seems to me that Sophie has both panic disorder and generalized anxiety disorder. I want to talk to you about some medication options if Sophie is open to it."

I see my mom's eyes well with tears. She hates to see me suffer and clearly had no idea how bad it had become.

"How do you feel about medication?" Dr. G asks me.

"I'm nervous, but if it will get rid of my anxiety, I'll try it."

"What about medication makes you nervous?"

"I don't want it to change who I am."

"If it works, it will bring out the best in you. It won't change you, but if it works, it will make you feel like a better version of yourself. And I'm going to be honest; that is a big 'if.' A lot of times, it takes a while for medication to work, and often it takes a few tries to find the right medication. I want to put you on a low dose of Prozac. And

I want you to have some Xanax for you to take if you feel like you are having a panic attack. Mrs. Riegel, is this OK with you?"

"Yes, it's totally fine. Is this OK with you, Sophie?" my mom asks me.

"Yes."

"It will probably take anywhere from four to six weeks for you to feel the effects. And you need to know about the side effects. This medication could cause fatigue, make you bruise more easily, cause dizziness and nausea, change your appetite, make you sweat more, and it can decrease your sex drive."

"I'm not worried about that," I say, smiling.

"Call me immediately if you notice any problems," he says, as he hands over his business card. "And plan to come back in two months so I can see how Sophie is doing."

I see my mom reach for the checkbook. Even though she tries to hide it from me, I see the check is made out for…a lot.

I immediately have a flashback to the first time I saw Dr. S's check. I take a deep breath.

Calm down. It's worth it. I'm worth it.

When I get home, I Google my medication (I clearly have not learned my lesson). Instead of freaking out, I'm excited. I can't wait to see if this will change my life.

Chapter Eight
Effects of Medication

I walk into Dr. S's office so excited to tell her about my new medication. It's been a week since I started taking it.

"Hey Dr. S!"

She smiles at me as I sit on the couch in her office. I notice that she is wearing a new bracelet, but I don't mention it.

"Hi Sophie. You seem extra excited today. Tell me about your week."

Where do I even start?

"I started medication this week. I'm taking Prozac and I feel *awesome*. Like a whole new person," I spit out.

Slow down. Don't talk so fast. Take a breath.

"That's great. I'm so happy for you. What feels different for you?"

"I feel really positive. And I feel like I can take tests without freaking out. I haven't had a panic attack in a week, which is really great. I feel like the voice in my head that is always looking for something to worry about is so much quieter."

"I'm glad you are feeling so good. I can't remember the last time I saw you smile this much."

"Thanks," I say, smiling.

"You said you've only been on it for a week?"

"Yes. But I know what you are thinking," I say, feeling smart, but also hoping that I actually do know what she's thinking.

"OK, what am I thinking?"

"You are thinking that it can't possibly be working yet, but it is. I'm serious. I feel so calm and I can finally breathe."

"Have you heard of the placebo effect?"

"Yes. I know, but I don't care. I don't care why it's working."

"I agree."

"And you know what's even better?"

"What?"

"I have midterms next week, and I feel great. Last year, I was a mess. But I don't feel anxious at all."

"That's great, Sophie. You deserve to feel good."

———

It's midterm week, and I have to study for five tests in total. (*Cue dramatic sound effects*). I make multiple color-coded study guides for each of my tests. (Don't ever discount the power of a pack of multi-colored highlighters and sticky notes.) After organizing each study guide by subject, date, and difficulty, I plow through my materials, memorizing facts and numbers and historical dates. Call it a placebo effect, Prozac, or amazing organizational skills: I feel really confident. I walk into my chemistry midterm (in the middle range of difficulty for me); everyone around me is freaking out, and for once, I'm not. Who cares if this midterm counts for two test grades, which is approximately 30 percent of my quarter average, which is an entire 7.5 percent of my overall average? Not me. That's for sure.

"We are going to fail," my friend says to me as we enter the classroom.

"We prepared as much as we could have, so there is no point in worrying now," I say.

Wow, I'm good. I should be a therapist.

I smile and sit down in a wooden desk.

Why am I not worried about getting a splinter? Why do I only have two pencils, not ten? This medication is freaking awesome.

As the test is passed out, I wait for my stomach to turn. I wait to hear the gurgling in my stomach that happens right before I throw up, but it never comes.

This is amazing. Now I can just focus on the test.

I look at the test and start. No hyperventilating. No shaky legs. No thoughts about failing or not being the valedictorian.

———

After I take all five of my midterms, I find that I am not obsessing about the answers or what I could have possibly answered incorrectly. I am so proud of myself, but more than that, I'm so happy I am on meds. What a difference they make.

As soon as I see Ms. F, I run to her to tell her about my medication.

"I started medication, and feel really good. Thanks for helping me through all of this."

"I'm so glad that this is working. I am always here for you," Ms. F says.

What did I do to deserve such incredible people in my life?

"Guess what?" I say to Ms. F.

"What?"

"I got a 97 or higher on all of my midterms!"

"That's great. You should be very proud."

———

After midterms are over, I can start to focus on winter track. I do the racewalk—an event you may never have heard of—and I'm really good at it. Last year, I beat a senior by fifteen hundredths of a second to earn my All-County title. And then, I made it to nationals. This year, I'm ready to go even further and make it to the state meet, become All-State, and go to nationals twice. The New York State qualifier meet is in two weeks and it's all I can think about.

"Mom, can I tell you something about my race in two weeks?"

"Sure."

I take out an index card from my pocket and hand it to her.

"What is this?" she asks.

"It's a list of all the people who will be at the meet and their times. I highlighted the people who I think can beat me."

"Honey, I think you're obsessing a little bit."

"No, I'm just strategizing. There is a difference."

"Why don't we talk to Dr. S about this, OK?"

I'm fine. I'm just excited. Maybe I'm obsessing a little bit, but it's not bad obsessing.

"OK."

The next day, I go to Dr. S.

"Hey, Sophie. What's going on?" Dr. S asks me.

"My mom thinks I'm obsessing over this big meet that I have next week."

"Are you?" she asks.

"I guess a little. But I don't think it is harmful. I think it's helping me prepare."

"You need to keep an eye on it because it is likely that these thoughts will become intrusive. Speaking of intrusive, how are you feeling now that you've have some time to adjust to the medication?"

"Really good, actually."

"OK, great, but please let me know if anything changes."

———

A week later, I come in first place at the state qualifier meet and feel on top of the world. I am so ready for the state meet. As a sophomore, no one expects much from me; I'm going to blow them all away.

The day before the state meet, I feel a bit anxious, which surprises me. Where did overconfident Sophie go? I need her *now*.

"What if I don't do well?" I say to my mom, hoping she will give me a pep talk.

"You will be sad, but that's it."

"Are you going to be disappointed in me?"

"Absolutely not. I'll be sad for you, but not because of you. You are going to go out there and try your best. That's all you can do."

"Yeah, I guess so."

"Well, I know so," my mom says. "I'll be there the entire time. I'm proud of you no matter what happens. This is an awesome opportunity that you have earned. No matter what, it is an accomplishment to be here, OK?"

"OK."

"Go get some sleep. You have to wake up early tomorrow."

————

Today is the day. I feel both exceptionally calm and energized. I had a dream that I came in seventh place, which would be *amazing*. I put on my uniform and pick out a pair of lucky socks. Then I pack up my track bag with extra deodorant, protein bars, my foam roller, and an extra pair of shorts in case mine rip.

When I get to the track, I don't feel like my stomach is going to explode. I'm still waiting to panic or cry but nothing happens.

"First call for the 1500-meter racewalk," I hear over the loudspeaker.

That's my event. Let's do this.

I go to the clerking area and see all of my competitors. I'm supposed to come in eleventh, based on our time rankings, which means I'm in the slower race, which means my race is first. I start to stretch and warm up, and then stand on the starting line. I feel a slight tremor in my knees and almost smile; I'll take these nerves any day.

You trained for this. Go get it.

"On your marks," I hear.

OK. Get ready.

The starting gun goes off. I'm out in front. After the first few laps, I have a big lead.

"Go, honey! Woooo!" my mom yells.

I would smile, but I have to stay focused. I give a thumbs-up to my family. They are cheering so loudly that it's embarrassing.

Two more laps. Come on.

"Push it!" my coach yells.

One lap. That's it. You got this.

I finish the race...and win.

I feel so proud of myself and victorious, even though I don't know the results of the other race. Ten other athletes are left. I need to beat three of them to come in the top eight. Top eight get medals and the title of All-State. I hear the gun go off. I watch nervously as they compete. I think that I am going to have a panic attack, but it never happens. They turn the corner to race-walk their last lap.

They finish. I look at the boards. I came in seventh place.

"I did it," I yell to my parents.

I run over to my coach and hug him.

"You earned this," he says. "You put in the work."

I want to tell him that I think it was the medication that helped me, but I don't. I mean, who knows? Maybe it was my medication. Maybe it was my hard work. Maybe it was luck. Or maybe it was all three. I don't care either way. I won.

———

For the rest of sophomore year, I take my medication happily and feel on top of my game. My grades are great. My races are great. My life is great.

Maybe this was me all along. Maybe I was meant to be this happy. Maybe my pledge to beat this in Aunt Nancy's memory is coming true.

———

On my first day of junior year, my mom yells up to me, like she does every year, "Honey, come down so we can take a picture."

She's so predictable.

"I'm coming," I say, putting on my jeans and blue t-shirt.

"Did you take your medicine?" my mom asks.

"Oh no. Not yet. Thanks for reminding me."

I take my medicine and a deep breath. I feel ready to take on the day.

My mom drives me and my brother to school. As we get closer, I feel a little bit nervous. My hands are shaky and my stomach gurgles.

It's OK, it's OK. Just typical first day of junior year nerves. Nothing I can't handle.

The day goes by fast. My teachers seem nice. All is good.

For the next few weeks, I really enjoy school. I am still seeing Dr. S, and while we have less to talk about, we still manage to fill the time. Dr. G is also really happy that I'm doing so well. I can't thank him or Dr. S enough. They have changed my life; I'm in school and not panicking.

———

A month into the semester, I walk into school, go to my locker, put my running shoes away, and go to my first-period class. I take out my math notes to study for the test I have today. As I sit down, I start to feel a bit dizzy.

Maybe I'm just hungry.

I grab a protein bar and eat it. As my teacher starts talking about acceleration due to gravity, my hands start to shake.

How am I supposed to take notes like this?

I take some deep breaths, but then my legs start to tingle.

This can't be a panic attack, right? I mean, I haven't had one in ten months. And I'm on medication. Maybe I'm sick.

I look around the room, searching for the nearest garbage can just in case. There's one by the desk in the front of the room, there's one in the back of the room near the lab tables, and there's one by the door.

My heart starts pounding. I'm sweating.

Am I having a heart attack? Oh my God. I'm having a heart attack. I'm dying. There's no other explanation.

"Can I go to the nurse?" I ask my teacher.

"Sure. Take a pass."

Where is the pass?

I try to ask but no words come out. I stand up and feel like I'm going to fall. I make my way to the door and walk slowly to the stairs.

Shit. How am I supposed to get down the stairs?

I take a step down the stairs and feel wobbly; I can't do it.

Find Ms. F. She will know what to do.

I walk through the science hallway and into the math hallway. Now my vision is blurry.

FIND MS. F!

I'm so close to her room. I hold on to the wall to steady myself. I reach her room and open the door.

"Hey Sophie. What's up?" she says.

"I can't feel my legs."

"Tough workout yesterday?"

"No, I really can't feel my legs."

My breathing is really heavy. I lose my balance.

"Oh. Sit down. Sit."

"OK."

"What's going on?" she asks me, clearly concerned.

"I don't know. I can't breathe. I can't feel my body."

My heart is racing even faster. Ms. F reaches out to touch my arm.

"Sophie, you are burning up. Take off your sweatshirt."

"I can't. I can't move my arms. I can't feel anything. I don't know what's happening. I think I'm having a heart attack."

"OK, just sit here. I'll call the nurse."

She calls the nurse. I can't hear what she's saying. All I hear is a buzzing noise.

"The nurse is on her way. I'm here, OK?"

I nod, but my eyes close.

"I need you to keep your eyes open. OK?" she says.

"What?" I say.

"Listen to me. Until the nurse comes, I need you to keep talking. Tell me about track. How's it going?"

"Good."

"What did you do at practice yesterday?"

"We ran."

"How far did you run?"

"I don't know. I don't know. What's happening? I'm scared. Don't leave me."

"I'm not leaving. The nurse is going to take care of you."

"I'm scared."

I look at Ms. F. She knows I'm scared. She knows what's going on, even though I don't. Just then, the nurse walks in.

"Hi honey. What's going on?" she asks me.

"I don't know. I can't feel my legs."

"You can't feel your legs? Like pins and needles?"

"I don't know. I need help."

Ms. F pulls the nurse to the side.

"She's having a panic attack," Ms. F says.

"OK."

The nurse looks at me and asks me, "Can you tell me what your name is and what grade you are in?"

I'm not in fucking kindergarten.

"Sophie and eleventh grade."

"Can you come sit in the wheelchair for me?" the nurse asks.

"I can't stand. My legs—they aren't working," I say, trying not to cry.

"OK."

She comes over to me. "Ms. F, can you help me get Sophie into the wheelchair?" she asks. They each take one of my arms and help me into the wheelchair.

"Am I going to die?"

"No. You are going to be just fine. I promise," the nurse says.

As she wheels me down the hall, Ms. F tells me that she will come check on me later.

As soon as I get to the nurse's office, I feel much better. Like a whole new person. I stand up and start walking around. I can feel my legs again. I can see clearly. My heart rate is normal.

"Sit down," the nurse says.

"I feel fine. Can I go back to class now?"

"Not after giving us a scare like that. We need to call your mom."

"Fine."

"Hi, Mrs. Riegel. This is the nurse at the high school. Sophie had a panic attack. She couldn't feel her legs, so we brought her here in a wheelchair. She says she is fine now. Would you like to speak with her?" The nurse hands me the phone.

"Hi, Mom."

"Hi honey. What's going on?"

"I had a panic attack, I guess. I tried coming down to the nurse but I couldn't feel my legs. But I'm fine now. Everyone is just overreacting."

"I understand that you feel fine, but you have to understand that it must have been scary for the nurse. You took your medication this morning, right?"

"Yes, I did. I haven't had a panic attack in months, so I don't know why this happened. But I feel better now."

"OK. Let's keep an eye on it."

"Do you think I will have another one?"

"There is no way for me to know. Let's talk about it with Dr. G when you get home."

"OK. Love you."

"Love you, too."

I hand the phone back to the nurse.

"Just take a seat, OK?" the nurse says.

I sit, but I'm not happy about it.

About an hour later, she lets me go back to class.

Oh my god! I still have a math test. I completely forgot.

I walk upstairs and run into Ms. F.

"I was just coming down to check on you," she says.

"Thanks. Sorry for scaring you."

"How are you feeling?"

"Fine. But I don't think I can take my test. Do you think my teacher will understand?"

"Go ask her. I honestly don't know what she will say," Ms. F admits.

"What do I say? I don't want to give a lot of detail. Only you really know everything about me. And it was hard to tell you."

"That's really up to you. You don't have to tell her anything, but if she asks why you can't take the test, you may have to tell her."

"Do you think she will believe me?"

"I don't see why not."

"OK, thanks," I say.

"And please come see me at the end of the day. I want to make sure you are all right," Ms. F says.

I smile. I love how much she cares about me.

"I will."

I walk down the hall to my math teacher's room. I look in the room and see she's teaching.

This cannot wait. You need to tell her now. You have a test in an hour.

I knock on the door. She waves me in.

"Can I talk to you for a second?" I ask.

"Sure. What's up?"

"I know you have a class right now, so I'll give you a short version. There's a really good reason why I can't take your test today. I can explain later, but trust me, it's a real reason."

Wow. I sound super suspicious.

"OK. I trust you. Take it tomorrow, OK?"

I take a deep breath and feel some color come back to my face. "Thanks so much."

"No problem, see you later."

I walk out of the room and see Ms. F.

"How did it go?" she asks me.

"She was fine about it. Besides you, my family, and a few other people, I'm not used to people being so nice about it. It was really nice of her to trust me."

"Yes, it was. I have to make some copies of this packet for my next class, but I will see you later. Come to me if you need anything. I'm always here for you." She smiles and walks away.

I feel fine the rest of the day. Maybe the panic attack was just some kind of fluke.

The next day, I take the math test without any anxiety.

———

Over the next few weeks, I start to have more panic attacks. Every day, I have at least one panic attack, and the days when I only have one are my good days. I start pulling my hair again. I bite off all of my nails. I grind my teeth so much that my jaw hurts. I cry every day, both in school and at home. I skip track practice because I don't have the energy to run after panic attacks. It takes all my mental energy to stay in school, but some days, I have to go home. I'm running out of absences. My mom is worried. Dr. S is worried. Everyone is worried, but I'm too busy worrying about having a panic attack to think about anyone else.

My mom calls Dr. G and makes an appointment.

"You may need to get some new medication," my mom says.

"I hate this. I hate my life. I don't know how much longer I can take this. I'm not going to commit suicide or anything, but no part of me wants to live like this."

"I know, honey. We are going to figure this out together. I made an appointment with Dr. G for later today."

"OK."

"Can I sleep in your room tonight? I don't want to be alone."

"Of course."

Later, we drive to Dr. G's office.

"Hey, Sophie. Tell me what's going on," Dr. G says.

"I have panic attacks every day. I can't take tests or run or do anything. I always feel like I'm dying, and I don't know why."

"Are you still taking your medication?"

"Yes."

"Sometimes medications only work for a certain period of time. It is possible that your body has gotten used to this medication and needs something different now. So, here's what we are going to do. We are going to try taking Xanax every day, not just when you are having a panic attack. We will see how that works, and then revisit the situation. But call me anytime, OK?"

"I have a question."

"What is it?"

"Do you think getting a dog would help? I've been thinking about it and I feel like a dog would keep me grounded and give me something else to focus on. Also, I've seen lots of videos of people with anxiety and how their dogs have helped them."

"It definitely couldn't hurt. What do your parents think?"

"They do *not* want a dog. But maybe you could tell my mom it would be good for me. I've wanted a dog for sixteen years."

"If you've been asking your mom for a dog for sixteen years, I'm not sure my recommendation is going to change anything. But I'll try. Let's get your mom in here and talk to her."

Dr. G tells my mom about my dog idea.

"Mom, a dog would be a great distraction. And it would teach me responsibility," I say.

"You are already sixteen and very responsible. Nice try."

"Well, I think it would help us all get more exercise."

"We all work out plenty already."

"And don't you want to give a dog a home? We could rescue a dog that had a bad home before."

"I like my clean, poop and fur-free home. Nope."

"We are such a loving family. I think that having a dog would be such a great distraction for me. I would be focused on the dog and not obsessing about other stuff. You know that's true."

"No. End of conversation."

"Fine," I say, knowing that this is definitely *not* the end of the conversation.

Chapter Nine
Hitting Rock Bottom

The first day I pop a Xanax, I feel a little bit weird, like I'm high (I've never been high, but I imagine this is what it feels like).

"Are you all right?" one of my teachers asks me.

"Yes, I'm OK."

My tongue feels like it is enormous. When I try to talk, it sounds like complete gibberish.

I decide to call my mom. "Hi," I say.

"Hi honey. Everything all right?" she says.

"My mouth. I can't talk," I say, sounding like someone who just got their wisdom teeth removed.

"What?" she asks.

I hang up and text her.

"I'm having some weird side effects from the Xanax. I'm super dizzy and I'm slurring my words."

"I'm so sorry, honey. I'm at work and so is Daddy, so I can't get you. Call your Uncle Jonny."

"OK."

A few minutes later, my uncle picks me up.

"So, how do you want me to tell your parents that you got high in school?" my uncle jokes.

I smile, because words are not an option right now.

When I get home, I nap for the rest of the day. I can't get out of bed. I feel like a zombie.

The next morning, I feel fine and take half a Xanax instead. But halfway through the day, my mind goes blank. Not the kind of blank where you just can't think of the right words to say, but the kind of blank where there are no thoughts at all. Nothing. It's like my mind is an empty space.

I skip track practice that day. I have no motivation to do anything. I go home and sleep. I don't do my homework or study for my tests. I don't recognize myself. I don't feel happiness anymore. I feel dizzy and disoriented. I start to realize why people cut themselves. They would rather feel pain than nothing. Pain is better than feeling empty. Anything is better than feeling empty.

Later that afternoon, I tell my mom that I'm not feeling like myself anymore.

"What do you mean, you feel nothing?" she says, concerned.

"I don't feel happy or sad. I feel like a zombie. I need to stop the medication. I hate it."

"OK. I'll call Dr. G."

"I think I would rather have panic attacks every day than feel like this. At least when I'm panicking, I feel something. I'd rather feel overwhelmed with emotions."

Later that week, Dr. G. has me stop taking the Xanax and suggests I come in to see him as soon as possible.

He ends up telling me that I should increase my Prozac dosage, but reminds me it will take a while to find the right dosage, and even if this is the right one, it will probably take over a month for me to feel better.

When I get home that day, I become hysterical. I totally and completely lose it.

"What's wrong?" my mom asks.

"I can't do this anymore. It's been almost three months and nothing has gotten better. I hate myself. Why do I have to have this disorder? I don't understand what I did to deserve this. I just want to feel normal again. Please help me."

"I wish there was more I could do to help. This must be so hard for you."

"I can't wait another month. I need this fixed now. I need to get a dog," I say, still crying.

"We talked about this. We are not getting a dog."

"Mom, I need something. I need something to take care of. I need to be distracted. I don't want to sleep my life away."

"Daddy and I will talk about it, but don't get your hopes up. For now, you need to go back to Dr. S on a weekly basis. And I will let your teachers know what is going on. OK?"

"OK."

The next day, I feel incredibly relieved to not take my Xanax anymore. I feel excited. I feel *something*. It's already working.

I have a test today, which should be fine. I always do well on tests. I walk into my classroom, and my teacher hands out the test.

You got this, Sophie.

I take one look at the test, and my mind goes blank. I look closer but my vision starts to blur.

No. NO. NOO!

My stomach churns. My legs shake.

I look at my teacher to get her attention. She walks over to me.

"Do you have a question about the test?"

"No. I can't see it. I'm not joking. Like I can't read what this says."

"OK. Why don't you take a walk in the hallway for a few minutes and take the test later?"

"No, I want to take the test now. I can't keep making excuses."

"Sophie, you can't see the test. This is not an excuse. Go take a walk. If you take the test now, you will fail, and then we are going to have bigger problems."

"OK."

I get to the hallway before I burst into tears. I bang my head against the lockers, hoping the pain will make me forget about my panic attacks. It doesn't. Now I'm panicking and my head is throbbing.

What the fuck is wrong with me? Why can't I just take a fucking test?

I'm crying harder now. I want to go home. I want to cry in private, but I can't. I'm in the middle of the hallway and the hall monitors have no idea what's going. They're just staring at me.

The buzzing noise of the ceiling lights gets louder. I'm on sensory overload. I run to the bathroom to get away from the chaos, squat down and cover my ears with my hands. I squeeze my eyes closed. I just want it to *stop*. I grab my phone from the back pocket of my jeans and call my mom.

"You need to get me," I say, sobbing.

"What happened?"

"Just come. Please."

"OK, I'll be there in a few minutes."

A few minutes later, my mom pulls into the school parking lot.

I get into the car, still crying.

"Honey, what happened?"

"I was trying to…"

"Trying to do what, honey?"

"Take a test. And I…"

I can't breathe; I'm hyperventilating.

"I can't understand you while you are crying. I need you to take some deep breaths with me, OK?"

"OK."

"Breathe in. Hold it for three seconds, and then slowly breathe out. Let me know when you are ready to talk."

A few minutes pass.

"I was trying to take a test and I had a panic attack. I couldn't even see the test. I take it back. Panicking is much worse than feeling nothing. I'm so tired. I just want to go home," I say.

My mom leans over and gives me a hug.

"I know this hug doesn't make anything better, but it's all I can do right now. I love you and I promise we are going to get through this."

I smile, the first real smile I've smiled in a long time.

"Thanks, Mom. I don't know what I'd do without you."

"Well, I hope you don't have to find out for a long time. Can you do something for me, though?" she asks.

I nod.

"You have to go see Dr. S tonight, OK?"

"OK."

———

After dinner, my mom drives me to see Dr. S. I tell her what's going on. She makes sure I don't want to kill myself, and then time's up. Forty-five minutes are up; more money spent. And I don't feel better.

When I get home that night, I go up to my room. I don't brush my teeth (I know, it's gross), I don't put on pajamas, and I don't tuck in Lammy. I get in bed in my jeans. My mom, knowing that I'm feeling pretty down, comes up to tuck me in.

"Do you want to talk to me about how you are feeling?" she asks.

"I feel hopeless. Everything feels so dark." I start to cry. My mom holds me.

"We are going to get through this," she says. "I know it doesn't feel like that now, but it will get better. Remember before you started medication last year, you felt pretty hopeless, also?"

"Yeah, but this is different," I say, sniffling.

"I'm not going to stop until we figure this out. OK? And you know how persistent I am. That's where you get it from. You are a fighter," she says.

"What if it doesn't get better? What if I feel like this for the rest of my life?"

"Let's deal with one thing at a time, OK?"

"OK."

My mom hands me a tissue. "Can you blow your nose for me?"

I don't mind that she's treating me like a little kid. All I need right now is my Mommy. I need someone to take care of me.

I blow my nose and hand my mom the dirty tissue.

"Thanks for the lovely gift," she says, smiling.

"You are welcome," I say, feeling a bit better. "Thanks for taking care of me."

"Honey, taking care of you is my most important job. No matter how old you get, you will always be my baby, and I will always take care of you."

"I love you."

"I love you more," my mom says.

"I love you the most," I say.

Did I mention I'm competitive?

"No, I love you the most."

"No, I love you the most," I say.

"OK, fine," my mom says.

"Wait, what?" I say.

Damn, she's good.

"Goodnight. I'm right downstairs if you need me," she says.

"OK, goodnight, Mom."

———

About a week later, my mom and dad leave me and my brother at home while they go grocery shopping. My brother and I start looking at rescue dogs online that are up for adoption. We both know we aren't getting a dog; still, we can't help but look. Ever since Dr. G mentioned it to my mom, I can't get the picture out of my mind of a furry, happy dog greeting me as I come home from school every day.

We send a few pictures of adorable shelter dogs to our parents for fun. No response. We send a few more, this time with captions like "I need a fur-ever home" and "I've had it ruff." No response. I send one more cute face to them, and write, "I hear you're the best Mom and Dad in the world! Won't you be mine?"

A few minutes later, my mom calls me.

Shit, I pushed it. I'm totally in trouble.

"Hi mom. Is everything OK?" I ask.

"Yes, everything is fine. If you and Jacob want to look at an animal shelter later today, we can go. But you need to call to make sure they are open, OK?"

What? This has to be some kind of joke.

"We are getting a dog?"

My brother jumps up when he hears me say that.

"Daddy and I have been talking and it is something we are seriously considering. We think it would be helpful for you."

"You guys are the best!"

"We know," she says. "We will be home in half an hour. Get ready to go."

"OK, we'll be ready."

I hang up the phone.

"WE ARE GETTING A DOG," I scream. "This is the best day of my life!"

"I know! I cannot believe that it's happening!" my brother yells.

The next thirty minutes go by impossibly slowly, and the car ride to the shelter goes by even more slowly.

As we pull up to the shelter, my heart rate skyrockets. Not in the panic attack way, but in the I'm-so-freaking-excited way. I walk in and see an adorable puppy.

"We have to look at this one," I say.

"Sweetheart, we don't want a puppy."

"We?" I ask.

"I don't want to house-train a dog," my dad says.

"OK."

For the next half-hour, we look at all the dogs. I keep looking for reasons why each dog would be perfect, but I can't find any.

"There isn't anything here that would work for us, Sophie," my mom says.

"So, are we not getting a dog?"

"No, we are. This just isn't the right shelter. We can look again next weekend."

I don't want to wait.

"OK."

All week, Jacob and I look at animal shelter websites. We find all of the dogs that we like. We want a medium-big dog who is housetrained and not super old. When the weekend finally rolls around, we go to another shelter and look at all the dogs. Jacob and I walk into the kennel and see fifty giant pit bulls staring and barking at us; it's overwhelming. When we leave the kennel, we tell one of the volunteers about the dogs we liked from the website.

"Those dogs are not for first-time dog owners," he tells us.

"None of them?" I ask.

"None of the ones you mentioned."

"Jacob, let's go back in and look," I tell my brother.

We walk back in, and all the dogs are barking. All except one. Her name is Whitney and she is a five-year-old pit bull. She looks calm and sweet, but mostly, she looks scared.

"Can we look at Whitney?" I ask one of the workers.

"Sure. Wait here."

After a few minutes, the worker walks toward us with Whitney. Whitney comes right up to us and starts licking my face. I get on the floor and pet her. My mom is scared (she's had a fear of dogs for her entire life). I'm so excited that I can barely contain myself.

"This is the one, Mom."

"Hold on. Daddy has to be here for this. I am not adopting a dog without Daddy," she says. "I'll call him." She called him. "Michael, you need to get here now. We found the dog for us and you have to meet her."

My dad says he's on the way.

In the meantime, I'm having the time of my life. Petting Whitney is so calming. All of my worries seem to go away. I feel like I've known her for my entire life. But mostly, I can't believe that it has taken this long to meet my soulmate. I know it sounds crazy, but she's my best friend.

"So, what's her story?" my mom asks the worker.

"She came here about two weeks ago. She was with a breeder who bred litter after litter with her. And then he abandoned her and tied her to a pole on the side of the highway. She just had puppies a few weeks ago, but she never got to meet them."

"Wow," I say, and feel even more love for her.

"The good news is that since we've only had her for two weeks, she doesn't know her name yet, which means you can name her anything you want."

"We have to name her with something starting with *N* for Aunt Nancy," I say.

"Nash," my brother says.

"For a girl?" I ask.

"Why not?" my brother says.

"Mom?" I ask.

"I like Nash," she says.

"Nash, welcome to the family," I say.

My dad finally arrives and meets Nash. He falls in love, too. That night, we take her home—our beautiful doggy.

I take her for a walk before we bring her into the house. When I come inside, I tell my parents that Nash is a very fast walker.

"*She's* a fast walker? You are a nationally ranked racewalker and you think *she* is fast? What hope is there for the rest of us?" my mom says.

I smile.

"Are you fine if we leave for fifteen minutes?" my parents ask. "We need to get a crate, some toys, and a bed."

"Yes, I'm fine."

They leave and it is just me and Nash. Two complete strangers, now sisters.

"OK, Nash, it's just you and me, kid," I say. "You are going to like it here. Word of advice: my mom is the sucker. Give her some puppy dog eyes and she will feed you. But it might take a while. She's scared of dogs. But I know you understand."

I walk her upstairs to my room, and she comes onto my bed with me.

"Nash, I have to admit something to you. I have anxiety and that means that sometimes, I will need you to distract me. Sometimes, I will need you to lick my face until I stop crying. Sometimes, I will need you to remind me how lucky I am to be here. Can you do that for me?"

She doesn't answer (rude, right?).

"And Nash? I know you don't know me that well yet, but I love you. I know that you are exactly what I need, and I promise that on my darkest days, I will still love you."

Nash looks at me with her big brown eyes. I kiss her head and put a blanket over her and she falls asleep next to me.

"Sorry to wake you up, Nash, but I have to tell you something. I know that you were abused before you came here. And I want to promise you that that will not happen here. I know we both have some healing to do. I'll help you if you help me. You can trust me. I can't wait to start a new life with you. Does that sound good to you?"

Nash falls back asleep in my arms, snoring.

"I'll take that as a yes, Nash."

Chapter Ten
A New Beginning

I know I'm a nationally-ranked racewalker, but walking an eighty-pound pit bull who likes to chase squirrels and cats is a new kind of training for me. It's perfect, though, because I have the state championships in a little over a month.

It's 5:55 a.m. As soon as Nash hears the jingling of the leash, she wakes up, stretches, and, I swear, smiles. Her tail is wagging like crazy. She's so happy.

"Good morning, Nashie. Are you ready for a walk?"

She jumps on me out of excitement.

"Hmmm. I'm not sure if you want to walk. You don't seem excited," I tease her. "OK, sit, Nashie. I have to put your leash on."

I raise my hand up, and she sits.

"Good girl. Let's go."

We walk down the snowy street. I try not to slip, and then notice another person across the street walking her dog.

"Nash, do you want to make a friend? Come, let's go say hi."

As we walk toward them, the woman asks, "Is that a pit bull?"

"Yes. We just rescued her," I say, proudly.

"How can you live with that thing? Pit bulls are dangerous. Don't come anywhere near my dog with your dog."

My heart sinks.

"She's actually super friendly. Do you want to come pet her? She won't bite."

"Absolutely not. You should have left her in the shelter. That's where she belongs."

Her dog starts to bark uncontrollably as she whips around and jogs away.

Nash is oblivious to the insults. She just goes along her merry way, sniffing some yellow snow.

"Nash, you are the best dog. I'm sorry that you have to deal with this."

I pet her head, "Let's go back home and have breakfast, OK?"

———

Every morning, I look forward to our walks. Taking care of a living creature is a staggering responsibility that gives me hope that I can take better care of myself. I start to feel like I used to feel: confident, calm(ish), and energetic. The knots in my stomach slowly go away, and I can no longer hear the throbbing in my chest. Nash is my medicine and therapy; as much as I rescued her, she rescued me.

Getting Nash is by far the best thing to ever happen to me, but walking a dog daily in the dead of winter results in me catching a cold, causing me to miss an entire week of school. When I finally return to school, I'm told I have fourteen tests to make up. *Fourteen.* Four English tests, one essay, two history tests, one quiz, one physics test, one physics quiz, one business law test, one math test, and two Spanish tests. I'm completely overwhelmed.

For the next few weeks, I come home from school early because I'm having panic attacks again. I can't contain how overwhelmed I feel. It's all too much for me. I sit in my room and cry.

Nash comes up to my room and puts her paw on my lap.

"Not now, Nash," I say through tears.

She rolls over on her back, wanting a belly rub.

When I don't go over to her, she gets up, jumps on my bed, and lays down with her enormous head in my lap.

"Nash, I can't do this now. I don't feel well."

She senses something is wrong. Nash takes her paw and puts it on top of my hand. She insists that I pet her. So, I do. And my anxiety eases up. But I quickly start to cry again. I lean over to grab a tissue and Nash licks my face.

"Thanks, Nashic."

If she could talk, I'm sure she would say "Now that you are done crying, you can pet me, right?"

I lean my head against hers and follow the rhythm of her breathing. After a few short minutes, my heart beat slows. The two of us sit on my bed for a while, snuggling. Her warm, soft fur keeps me grounded.

———

It's the day before the state championships, and I'm not sure why, but I'm feeling calm. Honestly, I don't care why I'm feeling this way as long the feeling doesn't go away. I mean, I have normal pre-race jitters, but nothing I can't handle. I force myself to eat some eggs and cereal, and then I go to the stadium.

It's crowded with lots of parents, coaches, and athletes. It smells like a mixture of adrenaline and hot dogs. I walk over to my section of the bleachers and put on my bib number. I'm overwhelmed by the amount of people around me. There is no room for me to even sit. I walk toward the warm-up area, sit down for a few minutes, and just breathe. That's what Dr. S has taught me. Once I feel relatively calm and ready, I get up and start my warm-up drills and stretches. As other people run by me, my anxiety rushes in and I can't catch my breath.

"Are you OK?" the person sitting next to me asks.

I nod and quickly grab my backpack. I wave at my mom in the bleachers to get her attention. Once she sees me, I motion for her to come down.

"Everything OK?" she mouths.

"Just come," I say, trying to hold in tears.

"Let's go outside," my mom says.

I go outside with her and cry even harder.

"What's going on, sweetheart?"

"I don't know. But I can't feel my legs and my race is in ten minutes."

"Let's breathe together, OK?"

"OK."

We breathe together for a minute. I stop crying, but I still can't feel my legs.

"Mom, I feel like I am having a heart attack."

"That must feel really scary. Do you think you are nervous for the race, or is this something else?"

"A combination, I think."

I start to cry again.

"What's making you upset?"

"I've worked so hard for this and I want to do well so badly. I can't believe that this is happening now."

"I'm so sorry, honey. I know how hard you've worked. And you are going to do the best that you can do, and after the race, we will call Dr. G and let him know what's going on."

"OK. Thanks mom."

It's five minutes before the race and I go to the starting line. I feel dizzy and lightheaded. I see my coach standing next to the track, giving me a thumbs-up.

"Everyone, line up," I hear the official say. "One minute until the start."

I'm not ready. I can't do this.

"On your marks…"

I hear the gun go off and instinctively push forward. Elbows are flying everywhere, including mine. I finish the first lap and forget about my panic attack. I finish the second lap and start to feel a tingling sensation in my legs.

No. Not now.

A few seconds later, my legs feel like jelly.

What is happening?

I keep pushing.

Then, my vision blurs and my hands go numb. I close my eyes. My head starts to fall back. I catch it quickly, but I cannot open my eyes.

"Come on, Sophie! Only a few more laps," I hear my coach yell.

Then everything goes quiet.

I'm walking in circles but I can't see, hear, or feel anything. The only thing I know is that there is no coming back from this. As I approach the finish line, I start to trip over my feet. And once I finish, I collapse.

I feel someone trying to get me to stand up, but I can't hear what they are saying. I let them carry me off the track and into the medical tent.

"Can you hear me?"

I hear them faintly and nod.

"Can you open your eyes for me, please?"

I try to open my eyes, but can't.

"I need you to open your eyes. Otherwise we are going to have to take you to the ER."

I try again. I'm able to squint.

My parents are standing next to me.

"I'm going to take your heart rate and blood pressure now."

The young woman lifts my arm.

"Your heart rate is abnormally high, even if you did just finish the race. I'm concerned. Did you take any drugs before this?"

I shake my head no.

I open my mouth and whisper "sorry" to my parents.

"Sophie, why are you sorry? You did nothing wrong," my dad says.

I try to respond but can't.

A few minutes later, everything goes back to normal. I am able to open my eyes and speak.

"What just happened?"

"I think you had a panic attack," my mom says.

"Did I win the race?"

"No, sweetie."

My heart sinks, not because of the race, but because my body betrayed me.

"Can we go home now?" I ask.

"Sure," my dad replies. "I'll go get the car."

———

When I wake up the next morning, Nash is waiting for me outside my room. It's like she knows I need a little extra support today.

"Good morning, Nashie," I say, as I sit down next to her and give her a kiss.

Her tail wags.

"Do you want to go for a walk?" I ask.

Her face lights up as she jumps up on me.

"OK. Let's go."

I get her leash on and walk outside.

"So, Nash," I say. "I had a rough day yesterday. But I'm glad that I have you."

She sees a squirrel and lunges forwards.

"Come on, Nash. We aren't going to chase that."

She stops and looks at me.

"I love you, Nash."

When we get back into the house, I feel a little bit better. Even though I'm still devastated about my race, I feel hopeful. With Nash by my side, I feel like no matter what happens, I'll be OK. She will never be disappointed in me or judge me. That's something that you can rarely find in a person.

As I sit next to Nash on the couch, petting her as she takes her morning nap, my mom comes into the room.

"How are you feeling today?" she asks me.

"Honestly, I'm feeling better than I expected. Obviously I'm sad, but somehow, I feel lighter. Like a weight has been lifted off of my shoulders."

"I'm so glad to hear that," my mom says. "I do want to call Dr. G, though. I think he should know what happened."

"OK."

"Let's call him now," she says.

My mom dials the phone and leaves a message for him.

The next morning, he calls us back.

"Sophie, what's been going on?" he asks me.

"I had a big race yesterday, and as soon as it started, I couldn't feel my legs, and then I couldn't see anything."

"Has this happened before?"

"I've had some problems with my legs, but I've never lost my vision before. Except once during a math test."

"Your medication is supposed to help with your panic attacks. It's clearly not. I know this is frustrating, but we need to try something else."

"OK."

He prescribes lorazepam for me. While I'm annoyed that I have to start over, I have nothing to lose.

———

A week later, I have a national championship meet. I'm excited to compete with the support of new medication, but I'm worried that my body will betray me again. As the starting gun goes off, I feel a sense of calm. Everything around me fades away and it's just me. My form feels right. I focus on my breathing, staying as relaxed and controlled as possible.

I'm light. I'm fast. I'm strong.

I repeat this to myself over and over until I cross the finish line. I'm so focused on myself that I don't even realize I have won.

"Awesome race," my dad says.

"Thanks!"

"Aren't you excited? You are the national champion!" he says.

I'm the national champion? The freaking national champion? What just happened? This can't be real.

It really starts to sink in when I hear my name being called and someone places a gold medal around my neck.

"Nobody deserves this more than you do," my dad says to me.

I smile, knowing today I'm a winner in more ways than one, and that in the end, a mental health victory means more than anything.

———

"Mom!" I yell from the kitchen, as I'm looking through the mail.

"What's up?"

"I got an invitation to the school award ceremony. It doesn't say what I've won, but this is where they announce the Junior with the highest GPA. I'll know next week if I could be the valedictorian or not."

"Wow. You just made me nervous," my mom admits.

"I made *you* nervous? I'm the one with something to lose, not you."

"I know how much you want this and how much you've worked for this. So, I will be very sad for you if you don't get that award."

"I'll be very sad, too."

"Tomorrow, can you talk to Dr. S about it in your session?" she asks.

"Sure."

The next day, I go to Dr. S's office.

"Hey, Sophie," she says. "It's been a little while."

"Yeah, it has been."

"How have you been doing?"

"Honestly, the past few weeks have been tough for me. I've been in and out of school because of my panic attacks. The meet that I was telling you about a while ago happened, and I came in last. I had a panic attack during the race. I also changed my medication…and a few weeks ago, I won a national championship!" I say.

"Wow, Sophie. That's incredible. I'm sorry that you were unhappy with the outcome of the other race, but I'm so glad to see that you really pushed through."

"Thanks. Also, I want to talk to you about something specific today," I say, looking at the pigeons in the window.

"OK, what do you want to talk about?"

"So, you know that I want to be valedictorian, right?"

"Yes."

"Next week, I find out if I'm in the running. The Junior with the highest GPA gets an award, and I really hope it's me. But I'm really nervous about it. What if it's not me?"

"Let's play this out. Let's say it's not you. Then what?"

"I'll be devastated."

"OK. And then what?"

"Well, I've worked so hard. How could it not be me?"

"What are you really worried about?" she asks.

"People are going to make fun of me if it's not me."

"How much of this is in your control, Sophie?" she asks.

"All of it."

"So, you're telling me that you can control someone else's grades?"

"Well, no."

"So, it's not in your control, right?"

"Yeah."

"What *is* in you control?"

"I can mostly control my grades."

"Good. What else?"

"I can control how I react when I find out."

"Can you control how others react?"

"No."

"So don't put energy into something you can't control. It's a waste of time and it makes you miserable. Right now, there is nothing you can do except obsess over it. And obsessing over it won't change the outcome."

"You are right, as usual."

"And just so you know, if for some reason, you don't get the award, the people who really care about you won't care. Your family won't look at you any differently, and I hope you won't look at yourself any differently. You have so much going for you. This title doesn't define you. I've seen you grow up and mature since you were in seventh grade. And now, four years later, I can say confidently that you are going to change the world. You are an incredible person, Sophie. Don't let this one thing bring you down."

"That means a lot to me, Dr. S. I couldn't have done all of this without you."

"You are so much stronger than you think you are. I want you to remember that when things get tough. I won't always be here, but you have the tools to get yourself through anything."

"Yeah, I guess so."

"You guess so, or you know so?"

"I know so."

———

A week later, I'm sitting in my school auditorium with a few hundred other students and parents. Each time the principal calls a name for an award, I pray that it's not my name. Jacob's name gets called as the winner of the U.S. Marine Corps Academic Excellence Award. I am excited for him—and also relieved it's not me. I don't want any award besides highest GPA. I wait for two hours until...

"And the winner of the 2018 Asterean Award, presented by this year's valedictorian, is…"

Please say my name. Please. Just spit it out. The entire auditorium goes silent. All eyes are on me. I take a deep breath and close my eyes.

"Sophie Riegel!"

Oh my god! I did it! Three years of worrying and I did it.

With tears in my eyes, I get up to accept my award.

I look at my mom, who is sitting a few rows from the front, and smile. When I get back to my seat, I reach behind my seat, grab her hand, and squeeze it.

———

A few weeks later, after school ends, I sleep in and wake up to find my parents aren't home. Neither is Nash. I walk down the stairs and see a note that says "Went to the vet with Nash. Getting her anal glands expressed. Be back before 11:00. XOXO."

I make myself some breakfast when the phone rings.

"Hello?"

"Woof woof," I hear.

"Mom. That's not funny."

"Haha, OK. You are not going to believe what just happened at the vet," she says, and laughs. She starts laughing so hard I have trouble understanding her.

"What happened?" I ask.

"So, you know how Nash has been licking her paws a lot?" she says, trying to breathe through her giggles.

"Yeah."

"Well, the vet says it could be allergies," she says, "or that Nash has OCD." And with that, she starts roaring with laughter again.

"Is this some kind of April Fool's joke?" I ask, starting to laugh with her.

"No. I'm completely serious. But the funny part is that the vet said that dogs pick up these kind of traits from their owners."

"So, you are telling me that *I* gave *Nash* OCD?"

"Yup," my mom says, now hysterically laughing.

"So, the dog that was supposed to help me with my anxiety disorders now has an anxiety disorder because of me?"

"Yes."

"Oh my goodness. That might be the funniest thing I've ever heard," I say, joining her in uncontrollable laughter.

"I always told you that you were powerful," my mom says.

"She took care of me. I guess it's my turn to take care of her."

"I think we should get Nash a support dog," my mom jokes.

Oh, Nashie.

When they get home, I run over to Nash and give her a hug.

"Nash, we are going to get through this together. I know it probably seems impossible, but I'm living, breathing proof that it's not."

Chapter Eleven
Journal Entries

Craving Silence

'm so damn tired but I can't sleep. I lay my head down on my pillow and close my eyes, but as soon as I do that, my mind turns on. Like a siren, it blasts through my ears. And I can hear my heart beat. I tell myself that this is normal, yet I know that something is wrong but I can't do a thing about it. My anxiety is like fire. It burns me from the inside out and turns me into ashes. I'm running out of seconds in this minute to pretend I'm ok when I'm just craving some silence. Each minute lasts for what seems like an hour and it's because I am in excruciating pain. And yes, I can be in pain and I don't need to be bleeding to prove it. And just because you can't see it, it doesn't mean it's not there, because it is and it's real. And don't you dare tell me that I'm overthinking or being irrational because it is so real in my mind that it scares me sometimes. There are hummingbirds in my ears that won't stop flapping their wings for long enough so I can catch my breath. There are alarm clocks going off in my head, except I can never find the snooze button. I get no breaks from myself. And it takes me just under an hour to realize I have bitten off all my nails and my fingers are bleeding and I pulled my hair and I clenched my teeth so tightly that my jaw hurts. I don't even notice anymore that

I am rubbing my hands together until the skin peels off. And while I'm doing this, I am just trying to focus in on what you are saying and tune out the demons in my head, but they are louder. So I ask you to repeat things. And I ask you if I am doing ok because when you told me the first three times, I didn't believe you. I hope you can't tell that I am falling apart and I am losing the pieces to put myself back together. And I hope you don't believe that one day, there will be no pieces left, because I believe it and I'm terrified. I'm suffering. Hidden behind this smile is a girl who is afraid of her own shadow. I wake up every day knowing that as soon as I get up I have to fight to act "normal." I have to live knowing that there is no cure and that I will never stop struggling. I feel like I'm drowning in my own tears that no one else can see. The butterflies in my stomach are conspiring against me and are trying to eat their way out. And I'm still just here, sitting and thinking about the worst-case scenario for the day and it's only 5:55 a.m. I've been awake for a minute and my heart is already beating out of my chest. It's only been a minute, and it feels like a lifetime worth of suffering.

By My Side

A new chapter of life begins,

And I'm ready to embrace.

It all starts in spring.

And as the spring goes on,

And the flowers keep growing,

And I keep running,

And the birds keep flying,

It suddenly becomes too hot.

Not like cozy or even snug,

But just plain hot.

And then summer comes along,

And the people sleep too long,

And the birds sing their songs,

And the days become too long,

But something feels wrong.

Oh yes.

It's like a melting sensation.

I've been in this situation.

I just need some meditation.

But it doesn't go away.

It just stays there,

Like a bratty old pest.

So instead I embrace it.

Open up my door,

Let it sit on my floor,

But I'm feeling kind of sore,

So I think it wants some more.

But then fall rolls around.

Kind of cold but kind of sound.

Kind of round and kind of brown.

But I can see it's just not right.

I just hope for the next season

To come in soon.

But this time it takes even longer.

Finally, winter shows up.

Sort of cold and kind of tough.

It's a little bit too rough.

I think I've had just enough.

So I go back inside.

The pest is still on the floor,

Mocking me as I shiver.

So I ask:

"How are you not cold?"

And he says:

"I am controlling you; I don't feel anything,"

"What do you mean?" I ask.

"Let go of your fear and I will be gone," he said.

"Who are you?"

I ask, suddenly scared.

"Who are you?"

I yell.

"Who are you?"

I scream.

"I am OCD,"

He whispered.

And he never left my side.

Trapped

There is no light where I live.

It doesn't shine at all.

All there is is darkness.

I live without any light.

There are no sounds where I live.

I hear no noise at all.

All there is is quiet.

I live in utter silence.

There is no hope where I live.

I don't feel it at all.

All there is is agony.

I live in terrible pain.

There is no joy where I live.

I don't smile at all.

All there is is despair.

I live in awful misery.

There is no company where I live.

I am all alone.

All there is is me.

I live in painful loneliness.

There is no way out where I live.

I am trapped here forever.

All there are are locked doors.

I live with no escape.

Warning Signs

She smiled like she didn't have demons

She ran like she was free

She talked like she didn't know what darkness was

She wrote like she had curiosity that would last a lifetime

She danced like she didn't have a care in the world

But, she shot herself like she wanted to shout out that we had missed all the warning signs

She smiled because she wanted people to stop asking her if she was ok

She ran because she wanted to run away from her demons

She talked because staying silent became too painful

She wrote because she wanted to calm down the voices in her head

She danced because it was the only thing she could control

And she shot herself because I didn't notice that behind her smile, she was broken

Anxious Body

My lungs are screaming at me because they are running out of oxygen and it's all my fault.

My eyes are mad because the tears won't stop burning them.

My heart aches because I can't stop imagining my mom dying.

My feet hurt from walking in circles to try and calm myself down.

My ears don't stop ringing and my brain is blasting a siren that I can't turn off.

My jaw is sore from clenching my teeth to keep myself from screaming.

My fingers are bleeding everywhere because I cannot keep myself from biting them.

My head is pounding so hard, I think there's an earthquake.

My arms are scarred from all the times I couldn't help but pick at them.

My body is confused because my mind keeps playing tricks on me.

Everything Hurts

It hurts.

That I have no control.

It hurts so much more.

That I am trapped with no escape.

It hurts so deeply.

The visions in my mind.

It hurts like nothing before.

The torture that exists within me.

It hurts.

The painful thoughts that won't leave.

It hurts.

The lies that I've believed.

It hurts.

The lonely place in which I dwell.

It hurts unbearably now.

The life that I am living.

It hurts.

Everything hurts.

Perfection

Perfection,

So hard to obtain,

So easy to lose.

Perfection,

A common goal among humanity,

But one that can't be reached.

Perfection,

A non-existent dream,

Only exists within our heads.

Perfection,

Leads to failure and defeat.

Perfection,

The disease of the living,

The regrets of the dead.

Perfection.

Liars

They say the sun is out.

They say it's shining bright.

But I don't feel its warmth,

For I can't see its light.

They say the night is calm.

They say it brings them peace.

But all I feel is darkness,

And a yearning for night to cease.

They say the world is healing.

They say it's turning good.

So I can't make it better,

But if I could I would.

They say my heart's not broken.

They say that I'll be fine.

But I know it won't mend,

For I feel like I am dyin'.

They say I've found myself.

They say I've been through it all.

But I have no clue who I am,

And I know that I'll still fall.

They say that I've found love.

They say I'm not insane.

But I know that's not the truth,

For all I've found is pain.

They say that they are people.

People who wish to be like me.

But I know they're just liars,

Who are so damn lucky to be free.

Are you there?

Are you there? I wonder.

Because you left no trace.

Are you there? I scream.

Because I can't feel your presence.

Not a soul can hear me.

I am locked in.

And the darkness can't carry

Out my yell.

But I am still here.

Just waiting for you.

Oh, I am still here.

Just praying for you.

Where are you?

Away from me, I know.

Where are you?

Farther than I can go.

You've left me in pain,

More awful than you know.

It hurts.

The way you've walked away.

I need you,

To survive.

You are my whole world.

And by leaving you've collapsed it.

I am suffocating.

Come back.

Please.

Are you there?

Nobody answers.

It's Time

It's time.

Time to break free.

Break free from myself.

Break free from the pain.

Break free from the darkness.

Break free from the fear.

It's time.

Time to rebuild my strength.

Time to feel joy.

And time to live again.

So much time has passed.

But the past is behind us.

And the future is unpredictable.

So now is what matters.

No later, no earlier.

Only now.

It's time to get away.

It's time to reconnect.

It's time to escape the isolation.

It's time to make my move.

It's time to leave the darkness.

It's time.

PART 2

You

Chapter Twelve

Facts Versus Myths About Anxiety

Stigma surrounding mental illness is a major issue. But by debunking the myths about mental illness, specifically anxiety, we can reduce the stigma. Here are some commonly believed myths about anxiety:

MYTH: People have anxiety or panic attacks just for attention.

If anything, we try to avoid seeing anyone when we are having a panic attack because it can feel embarrassing and we may feel ashamed. Having a panic attack in public feels like being forced to strip in Times Square; you are completely vulnerable, you are being judged, and nobody will come to your rescue. Having a panic attack isn't "cool" or "fun"—it's terrifying.

MYTH: If you have anxiety, you should just avoid the situations that make you stressed.

To be completely honest, I used to believe this one. I have to remind myself every day that this is just a myth. While avoiding the situation that makes you anxious may feel helpful in the moment, it can actually be detrimental in the future. When you avoid the triggers and sources of your fears, you actually become more fearful, because you are convincing yourself that there is an emergency when there isn't. The next time you come across the thing that makes you anxious, your body will have an even stronger reaction because by avoiding the fear previously, you were reinforcing the idea that you need to be afraid.

According to Edward A. Shelby in *Psychology Today*, "Understanding negative reinforcement will help you combat fear in your daily life… Negative reinforcement in the case of anxiety can be thought of as 'avoidance.' Each time you attempt to accomplish a goal, but you let the fear take control and back down, you are avoiding and thus negatively reinforcing yourself."[1] The more you avoid the situations, the more likely you are to avoid those situations in the future.

MYTH: Anxiety comes in one form.

Everyone does *not* experience anxiety the same way. There are many different forms of anxiety, which is why you get diagnosed with a specific anxiety disorder, not just "anxiety." There are six major types of anxiety disorders, each with its own distinct characteristics and symptoms. These include generalized anxiety disorder, panic disorder, obsessive-compulsive disorder, phobia, social anxiety disorder, and post-traumatic stress disorder. In general, more women are affected by anxiety disorders

---

[1] Shelby, Edward A. "Avoidance of Anxiety as Self-Sabotage: How Running Away Can Bite You in the Behind." *Psychology Today*. Accessed October 10, 2018. https://www.psychologytoday.com/us/blog/overcoming-self-sabotage/201005/avoidance-anxiety-self-sabotage-how-running-away-can-bite-you.

than men. Women are twice as likely to have generalized anxiety disorder, panic disorder, and post-traumatic stress disorder.

My anxiety and your anxiety are not identical. If we all had the same anxiety, the same medication and therapy would work for everyone. Unfortunately, different anxiety disorders are often clumped together and just called "anxiety." That's like selling apples but not telling people what type of apple they are buying. Not all apples are the same. Some are red, some are green, some are yellow, some are sweet, and some are sour. Anxiety is the same way.

MYTH: Teenage anxiety is not a big deal.

Anxiety is a big deal at any age. On average, one in five teenagers struggle with anxiety. When untreated, anxiety disorders, especially in teenagers, can lead to substance abuse, self-harm, and depression. Because this myth is so commonly believed, many adolescents don't share the fact that they are struggling with anxiety and don't get the treatment that they need. According to the Nuffield Foundation, "The proportion of 15/16 year olds reporting that they frequently feel anxious or depressed has doubled in the last 30 years, from 1 in 30 to 2 in 30 for boys and 1 in 10 to 2 in 10 for girls."[2] This is not a negligible change and should absolutely not be ignored. Teenage anxiety is a really big deal, and it needs to start being treated as one.

---

[2] "Increased Levels of Anxiety and Depression as Teenage Experience Changes over Time." Nuffield Foundation. Accessed October 10, 2018. http://www.nuffieldfoundation.org/news/increased-levels-anxiety-and-depression-teenage-experience-changes-over-time.

MYTH: Anxiety is something to be ashamed of.

This is a very unfortunate myth that is being reinforced every day by our society. We are told to just be "happy" and to "put on a fake smile" so we don't seem sad or anxious. We are taught to be ashamed of our imperfections and to hide them; otherwise, we will be judged. We are told that just being ourselves isn't good enough. Let me tell you something: Whoever has been telling us that is a liar. There is no need to be ashamed of our anxiety.

First of all, you are not alone, because 25 percent of all teens have an anxiety disorder. Second, your anxiety doesn't define you. You are so much more than your anxiety disorder. While you may feel as if you will be judged for your disorder, people are far too busy worrying about themselves to think about criticizing you. I used to be ashamed. I used to feel like once I told someone that I had an anxiety disorder, they would think less of me. I thought that in their eyes, I wouldn't be "perfect" anymore. I now believe that after telling people about my anxiety, I have actually gained their respect. Being open and honest takes a lot of courage. In a way, you are letting people know that you have been able to accomplish everything you have with one hand tied behind your back.

MYTH: You can tell when someone has an anxiety disorder.

People with anxiety often hide their symptoms, making it even harder for people to tell that they have an anxiety disorder. And, just because you see someone who looks nervous, that doesn't mean that they have an anxiety disorder. Anxiety is sometimes a silent killer. It claws at you from the inside, so nobody can tell that you are suffering. Sometimes, panic attacks are also silent. While everything in your head is chaos, the world around you goes silent. Since we cannot always tell when someone has an anxiety disorder, it is so important that we are kind and considerate to everyone. You never know what someone else is going through.

MYTH: You need a reason to be anxious.

"What are you so anxious about?" I hear people ask me. When I tell them that I don't know what I am nervous about, this is their response: "Well, you must be nervous about *something*. There has to be a reason why you are so anxious." If you don't have anxiety, you probably don't understand that you don't need a reason to be anxious. Anxiety is like a landslide. It takes very little to start it, but once it starts happening, you can't stop it without being crushed by the falling rocks. After a landslide happens, it's very hard to figure out what caused it in the first place. Was it an earthquake, or was it just gravity? We can be anxious without knowing why and that's totally fine.

MYTH: Anxiety will get better over time if I just wait it out.

A lot of people, including me, have thought that they can just deal with anxiety on their own and that if they just wait, it will get better. I used to believe that eventually my anxiety would just go away, but in reality, it just built up and led to more pain and fear. If I had gotten treatment earlier instead of trying to "wait it out," I could have avoided years of severe anxiety. So, if you are thinking about waiting to see if your anxiety, or any other mental disorder, will get better over time, stop.

People often wait a long time before getting treatment. It does not get better over time without treatment. You need treatment to learn how to cope with anxiety, and this is not usually something that you can do on your own. Don't wait to get help.

MYTH: Anxiety attacks are visible.

While the stereotypical panic attack involves sweating, shaking, and other very visible signs, many anxiety attacks are actually silent. Although it may be silent, panic attacks are still paralyzing. What we can do, however, is learn to support each other and be more understanding even if we can't see exactly what is going on.

MYTH: It's helpful to tell someone with anxiety to "calm down" or "be logical."

Many people with anxiety know that their fears are irrational, which makes it even more frustrating. If you tell someone to be logical, they will probably get even more irritated. They know that their fears do not make sense, but their bodies and minds are still reacting as if they were rational. If I tell you that I'm afraid that my mom is going to get shot or that I can't write with the red marker because something terrible is going to happen if I do, you might tell me not to worry because that isn't going to happen. Trust me, I *know* that that isn't going to happen, but my mind won't let me fully believe it. As much as you tell me that I need to stop worrying, and as much as you tell me that I am being illogical, nothing is going to change. I will still worry, and additionally, I will now probably not open up to you about my fears because you weren't understanding and you didn't have empathy.

MYTH: People with mental illnesses have trouble handling school work, a job, and daily tasks.

Many people are high-functioning despite their mental illness. While many people do need help getting work done and functioning properly, this should not be generalized to every person with a mental illness. In fact, 18 percent of people with an anxiety disorder are considered very high-functioning.

MYTH: Anxiety sucks.

Anxiety *does* suck most of the time, but not always. Sometimes, anxiety can actually be quite helpful. Because of my anxiety, I always get my work done way ahead of time. Since I fear that I will not get everything done, I end up finishing weeks ahead of my peers. This gives me a lot of time when I don't have work to do. Also, my anxiety has made me far more understanding toward other people. I have become a much better listener. When my friends tell me about their problems, I am able to figure out what to say to them based on what I like people to say to me when I am worried. I know not to tell them that they have no reason to worry and I know that people really just want to feel like they are being heard. I have learned so much about myself and the world around me because of my anxiety. While anxiety is the worst feeling in the world, I wouldn't be who I am without it. Anxiety helps shape who we are. It doesn't have to make us crumble if we can learn to control it.

MYTH: You are going to suffer forever.

At times, it might feel this way. Sometimes it might feel as if the world knocks you down as soon as you get the strength to stand back up. Sometimes you might want to give it all up. But, I can promise you that you don't have to suffer forever. With the right treatment, whether it involves medication, therapy, both, or something else, things will start to get better. If you are willing to put in the work, anything is possible. If you believe you are going to suffer forever, you are giving yourself the perfect excuse to not even try. You are giving up before the fight has even started. You don't have to be in pain for the rest of your life. Every day that you tell yourself that you can fight the anxiety is another day closer to ending the suffering. While the anxiety may never go away completely, you do not have to be in agony from it anymore. There is always a better way out.

FACTS:

- Anxiety disorders are the most common mental illness in the United States, affecting forty million adults in the United States age eighteen and older, or 18.1 percent of the population, every year.

- Anxiety disorders are highly treatable, yet only 36.9 percent of those suffering receive treatment.

- People with an anxiety disorder are three to five times more likely to go to the doctor and six times more likely to be hospitalized for psychiatric disorders than those who do not suffer from anxiety disorders.

- Anxiety disorders develop from a complex set of risk factors, including genetics, brain chemistry, personality, and life events.

- Anxiety disorders affect 25.1 percent of children between thirteen and eighteen years old. Research shows that untreated children with anxiety disorders are at a higher risk of performing poorly in school, missing out on important social experiences, and engaging in substance abuse.[3]

- The following is the likelihood of developing an anxiety disorder at some point in your life. (Note that this is data on adults only.)[4]

  - Any anxiety disorder. 28.8 percent

  - Generalized anxiety disorder: 5.7 percent

  - Obsessive-compulsive disorder: 1.6 percent

  - Panic disorder: 4.7 percent

  - Post-traumatic stress Disorder: 6.8 percent

  - Social Phobia: 12.1 percent

  - Specific (Other) Phobia: 12.5 percent

---

[3] "Facts & Statistics." Anxiety and Depression Association of America, ADAA. Accessed October 10, 2018. https://adaa.org/about-adaa/press-room/facts-statistics. (Five bullets prior to citation reproduced from press room article)

[4] "Current Anxiety Disorder Statistics." Calm Clinic. Accessed October 10, 2018. https://www.calmclinic.com/anxiety/anxiety-disorder-statistics.

- According to the National Institute of Mental Health, the following is the number of people living with or who have experienced anxiety disorders in the past twelve months in the United States alone:
    - Any anxiety disorder: 40,000,000
    - Generalized anxiety disorder: 6,800,000
    - Obsessive-compulsive disorder: 2,200,000
    - Panic disorder: 6,000,000
    - Post-traumatic stress disorder: 7,700,000
    - Social phobia: 15,000,000
    - Specific (other) phobia: 19,000,000
- Roughly 50 percent of children who experience anxiety in their youth will go on to develop an anxiety disorder.
- Women are 60 percent more likely than men to suffer from most anxiety disorders.

Chapter Thirteen
For Parents

Hard Questions Answered by a Parent (my Mom)

What do you think are some ways parents should *not* handle a conversation with their child about mental illness?

Talking about mental illness isn't an easy conversation, even for those of us who are steeped in it personally and/or professionally. Here are a few reactions I think parents should avoid:

1. **Departing:** Walking out of the conversation
2. **Distracting:** Talking about other things because the topic makes you uncomfortable, or doing other things while your child is trying to discuss the issue with you
3. **Denying:** Not believing your child's experience or perspective
4. **Defending:** Making excuses for the symptoms or condition, or saying, "This must have come from _____" (insert someone or something other than you)
5. **Distorting:** Making the issue into a bigger deal than it is
6. **Discounting:** Making the issue into a smaller deal than it is

7. **Directing:** Telling your child what to do rather than exploring possibilities collaboratively

8. **Dramatizing:** Becoming highly emotional during the conversation

9. **Disengaging:** Shutting down emotionally and not listening

10. **Dwelling:** Ruminating about the issue

What are some helpful ways to talk about mental illness with your child?

Every child is different, as is every parent or primary caregiver. Therefore, every relationship is different. So, it helps to ask yourself, "What has worked well for us in the past when we've had to navigate hard topics?" That question is part of a process I love called *Appreciative Inquiry*—getting curious about what's working when it's working well. Chances are, you've had at least one conversation with your child that went better than you expected. Ask yourself about:

- The timing of that conversation

- The tone of that conversation

- The setting of that conversation

- Who else was involved

- What mindset you brought to it

- What behaviors you demonstrated that you're proud of

- How your child behaved in response that you're proud of

- What you value most about that exchange

See how many of those elements you might be able to replicate in this conversation. And of course, adapt and adjust anything that needs it—especially if that great conversation was when your child was five and is now fifteen.

In addition, I would suggest you do the following (assuming your child is capable of having a productive conversation):

- Share your intention for the conversation (such as learning more about his or her experience, being supportive, etc.).

- Ask your child what kind of help he or she is looking for from you (and you might also offer a list of options, such as brainstorming buddy, shoulder to cry on, be a resource, offer ideas, etc.).

- Share any outcome you're already committed to, such as, "I am committed to getting you help for this. What kind of help you want or need is something we can discuss together."

- Remind your child *out loud* that you love them no matter what, and nothing will change that.

- Listen with the intent to understand, not to reply. This includes listening for what is being said *and* what isn't being said. It also includes noticing body language, such as, "I notice that your fists are clenched. What's going on for you right now?"

- Ask open-ended questions and follow-up questions that feel supportive, such as, "What's that like for you?" rather than, "Why didn't you tell me sooner?"

- Be open to what your child thinks he or she wants and needs, and explore those options with an open mind.

- Remind your child about the outcome you're committed to and brainstorm possibilities together.

- Make some time-sensitive commitments and an action plan.

- Ask your child, "How will I know if you're having trouble? What will it look like or sound like?"
- Ask, "How can I get your attention about your mental health if other ways haven't worked?"
- Ask, "What should I say to you when you're having a hard time?"
- Ask, "What should I never say to you?"
- Ask, "Should we have a code word for when you're having a difficult time in a public setting?"
- Decide when you're going to have your next conversation.
- Thank your child for having this conversation with you.
- Ask what you did well in this conversation, and what you could do differently next time.

What would you say to parents who don't know what to say to their child who is suffering?

Tell the truth: "I have a feeling you're suffering, and I don't really know what to say. I love you, and I want to help you—even if my helping you means taking you to talk to someone who isn't me. So, while I don't know what to say, I do know how to listen. Will you share with me what's going on?"

What if your child doesn't want to get help?

It's possible your child doesn't want help, or doesn't think he or she needs help, or doesn't want help from you. And without help, he or she won't get better. I would honestly do whatever it takes to get them help. Some options might include:

1. **Offer choices:** "You can either speak with me, the school social worker, or a therapist outside of school. It's your call, but you need to pick one of them by the end of the week."

2. **Tell a story about someone they admire who struggled, too:** "You may not know this, but Uncle David had a lot of the same stuff going on that you're going through when he was your age. He did *not* want help, because, like you, he's smart and social and capable. But eventually he was willing to talk to someone when he saw his grades start to slip, and he got right back on track. I think you could have a similar situation. What do you think?"

3. **Play hardball:** "I love you and I realize that I want more for you than you want for yourself right now. So, until you agree to get some help, here are some consequences..."

4. **Outsource the conversation.** Ask a favorite friend, relative, teacher, or coach to approach your child.

5. **Get curious.** "I think you're sadder than you need to be. You think you're the right amount of sad for a teenager. I'm not a teenager, so I'd like to understand your perspective. Will you share yours, please?"

6. **Get help for yourself.** Your child may not accept help, but you can both model accepting help and benefit from advice from a professional on what to do. Start with yourself.

What general advice would you give to parents?

You don't always have to know what to say or do because there's no one right way to handle mental illness—and things will change over time. Be compassionate, curious, available, and flexible. Be an advocate for your child and for yourself. And be yourself.

Interview Questions between Sophie and Mom (FOR PARENTS)

What do you think parents misunderstand about mental illness?

I got lucky. I mean really lucky. But even though my parents understand a lot about my mental illness, they don't understand everything (nor can I expect them to). And a lot of parents don't have any experience or education on the topic—or they're misinformed. I think that a lot of times, especially with anxiety, parents think that their kid must be worried about *something*. Sometimes, anxiety or depression is about nothing at all, or about everything. Parents often do not understand that if we don't come to talk to you, it may be for other reasons other than we don't trust you. Maybe we are ashamed. Maybe we just don't know what to say. Maybe we are talking to a friend instead. Maybe you didn't ask us how we were feeling and we didn't want to cause problems by telling you. Maybe we just don't want to. I'm not a parent, obviously, but I can imagine that parents may blame themselves if their child does not want to talk to them. Still, a lot of the times, it is not personal.

What should a parent say or not say if they think their child needs help?

What to say:

- "How can I help you?" Make sure your child feels like you are here for him or her.

- "I wish there was more I could do to help you." Even if you don't know how to help, it's nice to know that you want to.

- "Is there something that I am doing that is contributing to your feeling this way?" This is a great alternative to "What am I doing wrong? I didn't raise you to be mentally ill," or "Why are you so screwed up? Was it something I did?"

- "I'm here for you." Simple, but it works.

- "I'm sorry you are dealing with this. You are so strong." Compliments never hurt.

- "Can I give you a hug?" Always ask before, because sometimes the answer is no.

- "I don't understand what you are going through, but I would love to hear how you are feeling. Maybe we could learn about this together."

What *not* to say:

- "Why are you feeling _____?" With mental illness, especially with anxiety and depression, often what we are feeling is about nothing at all. Or maybe it's about everything. But more often than not, at least for me, there is no rhyme or reason for the way I'm feeling.

- "Maybe this is just a phase." It is not "just a phase." That feels very minimizing.

- "Just smile." Unless you have personally experienced a mental illness, you may not know that this is something no one wants to hear. It's the equivalent of telling someone who just got shot to put on a bandage.

- "In a few days, you won't even remember this." Focus on the present. We need you here and now. When you struggle with mental illnesses, it is hard to think ahead when you are suffering in the moment. So be with us in the moment.

- "You always get over this. You are fine." Again, this is minimizing. And in the moment, it is hard to believe this. This time seems different.

- "You just need to get out more. Maybe if you exercise more, you will feel better."

- "You are overreacting."

- "Do you know how bad you make me feel when you won't talk to me?" Two problems here: First, not only are we upset or anxious about ourselves, now we know we are upsetting someone else. That's not what we need. Second, sometimes we just don't want to talk about it. It's nothing personal—don't make us feel bad about it.

- "There is nothing to worry about."

- "That doesn't make any sense."

- "Don't bother me with your problems."

- "Relax."

What do you wish your parents had done differently?

I wish that my parents had suggested medication much earlier. I believe this would have helped me tremendously. But other than this, my parents did everything right. They gave me space when I needed it, they talked to me openly about how they were feeling, and they always listened to me.

What should teachers and other school administrators know?

The most important thing that teachers should know is that if a student comes to them for help, it is not easy. Take us seriously and talk to us like we are adults, not children. Teachers, in my opinion, often forget that students have lives outside of school. Sometimes, our lives are chaotic and we may need extra support, so please be understanding.

What can parents do to reduce stigma?

Parents should learn to talk openly about mental illness. Instead of saying to your child, "You know that thing that's been bothering you…" they should name the disorder. Say, "I want to talk you about your OCD," or "…your anxiety." Parents can also share articles with their child and educate other parents when they hear them talking about mental illness. Parents have to be advocates for their children, and there is no way to do that without learning the proper terminology and asking questions.

Chapter Fourteen

For Teens
(Questions Answered by Me)

What do you think teens misunderstand about mental illness?

I often hear "That's so OCD," or other phrases like that. I think kids often do not understand the gravity of what they are saying. They often joke about mental illnesses as well as suicide, which only creates an environment in which people feel as if they cannot express themselves. Also, teens may not understand that their feelings or behaviors may actually be mental illnesses. It is very important that teens continue to ask questions and express their feelings, even if their feelings feel "wrong" or "weird."

If a teen doesn't want to get help, what would you tell him or her?

If a teen doesn't want help, I would ask for the reason. Is it because of embarrassment or shame? Is it money-related? Is it because the teen doesn't think help is needed? I would also remind teens that they can always stop getting help once they start if they don't feel comfortable, but that if they never start to get help, they will continue to struggle.

What's the upside of mental illness?

When you have a mental illness, you learn how to be resilient immediately. And this carries over to everything that happens in life. You know what it's like to be at your worst, so you can appreciate the days when you feel really good. In addition, you learn that you can get through anything. People without mental illnesses oftentimes have not been challenged in the way people with mental illnesses have. People with mental illnesses know their strengths and weaknesses and are amazing advocates for themselves and others. They are also often more in tune with other people's emotions. Having a mental illness is the hardest thing to combat, but it is also rewarding, and honestly, I wouldn't change the way I am. I am a great friend because of my mental illnesses. I am a hard worker. I am passionate. I am strong. And so are you.

What are your highest hopes for reducing stigma?

- **I want those with anxiety to know that there are ways to strive and thrive, not only *despite* anxiety, but because of anxiety.** You may not realize that while anxiety can be disabling and may not feel advantageous, anxiety can also be a powerful force that can be used positively. I want everyone to know that those with anxiety can be high-functioning and just as successful, if not more successful, than anyone else. For example, did you know that Emma Stone talked about having panic attacks when she was a kid? Also, Johnny Depp, Scarlett Johansson, and Adele have all shared their experiences with panic disorder. And can you guess who else has an anxiety disorder? Here are just a few people: David Beckham, Drew Barrymore, Jim Carrey, Kate Moss, Miley Cyrus, Nicole Kidman, Oprah Winfrey, and Paula Dean. Can you guess what all these people have in common besides their anxiety? *They are all successful.* They are proof that anxiety doesn't have to limit your potential. You are not alone in the fight, and you are certainly able to accomplish whatever you want, both despite and because of your anxiety.

- **I want those who are trying to help to actually know how to help.**

  When I am in the middle of an anxiety or panic attack, the last thing I want to be told is to relax. But, the person who is trying to help doesn't know that. One reason, I know, why many times people do not know how to calm someone else down is because they have no idea what intense anxiety feels like. No one wants to be told that you are worrying for no reason or that you should stop worrying and calm down. If everyone in our society knew what to say or do to actually help someone with anxiety, we wouldn't need this book.

- **I want people to know that there is no shame in talking openly about mental health and mental illness.**

  Stigma related to mental health is a huge issue. Mental health stigma is a major problem, and much of it is caused by a lack of education. Also, the media often portrays those with mental illnesses as being violent and show that people with anxiety have trouble functioning in society, but this is not the case at all. And because of this stigma, if you have a mental illness, you may have to deal with bullying. I was bullied for years because of my anxiety. My classmates used to mimic my shaking legs and my tapping fingers. They also would chase me around with red markers, which was one of my irrational fears. The only way to stop the stigma is to talk openly about mental health. By reading about my battle with anxiety and how I came out about it despite my fear that my friends, family and teachers would desert me, I hope people of all ages will gain the courage to speak out about their own struggles.

- **I want people to know that asking for help doesn't make them weak.**

   Many of us with mental disorders avoid getting the help that we need because we think that it means that we are "weak." We may think that admitting that we need to talk to a therapist means that we can't take care of our own problems or that if we need medication, there is something wrong with us. But, as hard as it is, the first step to treating the problem is admitting that there is a problem. One of the hardest things for me as a twelve-year-old was admitting to myself that I was flawed, and that that is OK. I told myself to keep being perfect, but what I didn't know is how impossible that is. I never used to ask for help because I thought that I could handle anything. But sometimes, the best thing to do is ask for support. Getting help doesn't make me weak; rather, it makes me smart for realizing that my problem is too big to handle on my own. Admitting that I needed help was actually the best thing that I have ever done because without that help, I don't know if I would be where I am today.

- **I want people to know that it gets better.**

Despite my anxiety, I have succeeded in many aspects of my life. I'm an All-American racewalker. I have greater than a 4.0 grade point average in school. I have earned thousands of dollars in scholarships, such as science research awards and an anti-bullying award. I am an amazing sibling to my twin brother (but please don't ask him to confirm this). And I'm about to be a best-selling author. Also, with years of work and therapy, I have been able to learn how to control my anxiety. I want to give the mental illness and anxiety community hope that the pain can be temporary. It is important that we understand that, with some support, a lot of work, and this book, anxiety does not have to take over our lives. Everyone should see that while anxiety is painful and controlling, I have learned how to manage it and ultimately, I now know that it is possible to quiet the anxious voices in your mind.

Chapter Fifteen
Resources

For Teens

Active Minds: Active Minds is the nation's premier nonprofit organization supporting mental health awareness and education for students. "We are dedicated to saving lives and to building stronger families and communities. Through education, research, advocacy, and a focus on students and young adults ages fourteen to twenty-five, Active Minds is opening up the conversation about mental health and creating lasting change in the way mental health is talked about, cared for, and valued in the United States."[5]

Minding Your Mind: "Minding Your Mind's (MYM) primary objective is to provide mental health education to adolescents, teens and young adults, their parents, teachers and school administrators. Our goal is to reduce the stigma and destructive behaviors often associated with mental health issues. Treatment is available, yet only 3 out of 10 individuals needing help actually seek help. Minding Your Mind Programs move away from crisis based response to prevention through education.

---

[5] https://www.activeminds.org/about-us/our-story/

"Our educational programs provide information regarding signs and symptoms of these disorders, in addition to stressing that they are treatable and treatment is available. Mood disorders have been identified by the World Health Organization as the third leading cause of disability worldwide. Research studies have demonstrated that over 90% of people that die from suicide have one or more psychiatric disorders at the time of their death. The second leading cause of death of individuals between the ages of 14-23 is suicide. Since the age of onset of most psychiatric disorders is typically during adolescence, it is essential that the proper information be brought to the attention of secondary school educators, counselors, students and their parents. MYM offers several programs for students, teachers, faculty and the community at large."[6]

Student Mental Health: A Guide to Identifying Disorders and Promoting Wellness: "Going to college is a dream for millions of Americans, yet those with psychiatric disabilities may question if it's even a possibility. While mental illness may add extra considerations to the process of attending college, there are many options available to turn this goal into a reality. Current college students utilize campus mental health services more than any generation before them, showing that students are taking charge of their mental health and that colleges have services in place to help. In this guide, learn more about common mental illnesses, support systems, and how to request accommodations."[7]

---

[6] https://mindingyourmind.org/who-we-are/mission/

[7] https://www.affordablecollegesonline.org/college-resource-center/college-student-mental-health/

The Jed Foundation: "Transitioning into adulthood can bring big changes and intense challenges. The Jed Foundation (JED) empowers teens and young adults with the skills and support to grow into healthy, thriving adults."[8]

Here.Now.: "A teen-driven Jewish movement to provide support, build connections, increase wellbeing and resilience, and reduce stigma around mental health. Teens can engage in creative activities, partnerships, events, and innovate online content designed by teens for teens."[9]

Sources for OCD

International OCD Foundation: "The mission of the International OCD Foundation is to help everyone affected by obsessive compulsive disorder (OCD) and related disorders to live full and productive lives. Our aim is to increase access to effective treatment, end the stigma associated with mental health issues, and foster a community for those affected by OCD and the professionals who treat them. The International OCD Foundation is a donor-supported nonprofit organization. Founded in 1986 by a small group of individuals with OCD, the Foundation has grown into an international membership-based organization serving a broad community of individuals with OCD and related disorders, their family members and loved ones, and mental health professionals and researchers around the world. We have affiliates in 25 states and territories in the US, in addition to global

---

[8] https://www.jedfoundation.org/who-we-are/

[9] https://www.myjewishlearning.com/here-now/

partnerships with other OCD organizations and mental health non-profits around the world."[10]

Sources for PTSD

National Center for PTSD: "The National Center for PTSD is dedicated to research and education on trauma and PTSD. We work to assure that the latest research findings help those exposed to trauma."[11]

Sources for Suicide Prevention

American Foundation for Suicide Prevention: "Established in 1987, the American Foundation for Suicide Prevention (AFSP) is a voluntary health organization that gives those affected by suicide a nationwide community empowered by research, education and advocacy to take action against this leading cause of death.

AFSP is dedicated to saving lives and bringing hope to those affected by suicide. AFSP creates a culture that's smart about mental health by engaging in the following core strategies:

- Funding scientific research
- Educating the public about mental health and suicide prevention
- Advocating for public policies in mental health and suicide prevention
- Supporting survivors of suicide loss and those affected by suicide in our mission"[12]

---

[10] https://iocdf.org/

[11] https://www.ptsd.va.gov/

[12] https://afsp.org/

1-800-273-TALK (8255) National Suicide Prevention Lifeline:
"We can all help prevent suicide. The Lifeline provides 24/7, free and confidential support for people in distress, prevention and crisis resources for you or your loved ones, and best practices for professionals."[13]

Other Resources

- National Alliance on Mental Illness (NAMI): 1-800-950-NAMI (1-800-950-6264)
- Anxiety and Depression Association of America (ADAA): 1-240-485-1001
- National Institute of Mental Health (NIMH): 1-866-615-6464
- Centers for Disease Control and Prevention, Division of Mental Health (CDC): 1-800-CDC-INFO (1-800-232-4636)
- American Psychological Association: 1-800-374-2721
- American Psychiatric Association: 1-800-357-7924

---

[13] https://suicidepreventionlifeline.org/

Appendix

Acknowledgments

I would first like to thank Wendy Shanker, who encouraged me to write this book and never doubted me for one minute. She gave me the enthusiasm and spark I needed to continue along this journey.

Next, I would like to thank Kimberlee Auerbach Berlin, my editor and biggest supporter. She believed in the power of my story and never let me forget how meaningful this book is. I am truly grateful for her devotion to helping me share my story, and for her always treating me like an adult, even though I am a teenager. Day in and day out, she motivated me to keep on writing, and she always checked in on me to make sure that I still felt invested in this book. Her honest feedback and our long phone calls about edits were invaluable. Without her, there is no way this book would be published.

Someone who doesn't even know how much she helped me is my high school guidance counselor, Melissa Leder. She created a free period for me sophomore year so that I could have time to write every day. She listened to me when I felt anxious about sharing my story, and always reminded me that she would support me no matter what. Her kindness and willingness to take time out of her day to make me feel a little less nervous is something that I've never experienced before. She put me before herself many times, and she taught me that I could trust her with anything.

My therapist, Dr. Jean Schlegel, has helped me tremendously. Not only has she been supportive of my writing, but she has also continued to push me out of my comfort zone, even when I did not want to go. Because of her, I have grown and learned more about myself than I could have ever imagined. I would not be the person I am today without her.

My psychiatrist, Dr. John Sawicki, gave me hope when I was at my lowest point. I am forever grateful for his constant phone calls checking in on me and for him never giving up on me, no matter how much I thought I would never get better.

The most important people I need to thank are my parents and brother. I'm impressed, to say the least, by how gracefully they put up with me constantly doubting myself or needing reassurance just one more time. My mom has always been my biggest advocate. From letting me wake her up in the middle of the night because I felt lonely to always telling me she loves me, my mom is the reason why I know what unconditional love feels like. My dad was always the logical one, which our family desperately needed. He tried to rationalize irrational thoughts and feelings, but began to understand that all I needed was a tight squeeze and a kiss on the head. My dad is the reason why my panic attacks don't leave me feeling defeated anymore. Thank you to my brother, Jake, for always sticking by my side, no matter how annoying I may have been.

Lastly, I want to acknowledge my readers. This book has not been easy to write, and sharing my story is the most difficult thing I have ever done. Without my readers, there would be no purpose to my book, and I sincerely hope that my readers finish this book feeling inspired.

About the Author

Sophie Riegel is not your typical teenager. She's an All-American racewalker (who stands four feet, eleven inches), enjoys solving math equations and Rubik's Cubes, and has written a book about her struggles with anxiety. Sophie is the president of the board of directors for Here.Now., a mental health advocacy organization, and she strives to make a difference in the lives of those around her. She lives with her parents, twin brother, and rescue dog, Nash.

Made in the USA
Middletown, DE
12 April 2019